ON THE WALL
WITH HADRIAN

On the Wall with Hadrian
1st Edition
May 2006

Published by Eye Books Ltd
8 Peacock Yard
London
SE17 3LH
Tel: +44 (0) 845 450 8870
website: www.eye-books.com

Set in Garamond and Aldus by Peter Scott at Eye Books
ISBN: 9781903070499

British Library Cataloguing in Publication Data
A catalogue record for this book is available from the British Library

Printed and bound in Great Britain by Creative Print and Design

Cover design by Marina Asenjo at Eye Books

ON THE WALL
WITH HADRIAN

Bob Bibby

Published by Eye Books

Other books by Bob Bibby

Travel

Grey Paes and Bacon: From the Heart of the Black Country
Dancing with Sabrina: The River Severn - A Journey from
Source to Sea
Special Offa: A Walk along Offa's Dyke

(Published by EyeBooks)

Crime Fiction

Be a Falling Leaf
Bird on the Wing
The Liquidator
The Llareggub Experience

(Published by Pierrepoint Press)

Acknowledgements

Thanks to the following: Colin Brownlee, Helen Little, Sandra Maughan, Val and Sarah Gibson, Sue Hatt, Julie Glease, Janice and Dave Wiseman, Pauline and Ron, John and Kevin.

Thanks to the following for permission to quote from their translations: David Camden for Hadrian's poem about Borysthenes, Alan Bowman and David Thomas for the Vindolanda tablets, Rolfe Humphries and Indiana University Press for Ovid's Art of Love, the estate of H.Mattingly and S.A.Handford for The Agricola and The Germania by Tacitus (Penguin Classics 1948, revised translation 1970, reproduced by permission of Penguin Books Ltd), Robin Campbell for Letters from a Stoic by Seneca (Penguin Classics 1969, reproduced by permission of Penguin Books Ltd), Owsei Temkin for Soranus' Gynecology 1991 (reprinted with permission of The Johns Hopkins University Press)

Special thanks to Dr David Breeze and to Chris and Sandra Knights who read and commented helpfully on earlier versions of this text. Errors of fact, judgement or opinion are, of course, all my own.

"To Sol"

Contents

(Hadrian) was the first to build a wall, eighty miles long,
to separate the Romans from the barbarians.

The Life of Hadrian: Anon

Over the heather the wet wind blows
Lice in my tunic, a cold in my nose
The rain comes falling out of the sky
I'm a soldier on the wall and I don't know why

Roman Wall Blues: W.H. Auden

Verily I have seene the tract of it over the high pitches and steepe
descents of hilles, wonderfully rising and falling.

Britannia: William Camden

PROLOGUE

There wasn't much call for Latin-speakers in Wolverhampton in 1953. Come to think of it, there never had been, because the Roman army missed out on the opportunity to witness the world's greatest football team, the mighty Wolves, by marching past to the north on Watling Street. So it was a bit of a surprise when, on the first Tuesday of September in that year, the Reverend Frank Rust burst through the classroom door of the Grammar School and announced to me and my 29 fellow-pupils that he was going to teach us how to conjugate the Latin verb *amo* (I love). I was eleven years old and it was the first day of my inculcation into the mysteries of Greece and Rome that, unknown to me at the time, were to dominate my intellectual growth for the next ten years.

Still, such was my unquestioning acceptance of the ways of the world that this all seemed perfectly normal at the time. True, it was not easy to talk Latin at home or on the terraces at the Wolves' Molineux stadium or at the church youth club or anywhere else I went in the course of my daily life, but then you couldn't do algebra in any of those places either. But what the hell! Elizabeth had just been crowned, Sir Gordon Richards had just won his first Derby on Pinza, and Hillary 'n' Tenzing had just become the first men to conquer Everest. The least I could do, in the spirit of this new Elizabethan Age that was just dawning according to the *Daily Mail*, was to buckle down and learn to conjugate *amo*.

It was only ten years later towards the end of my Classics degree course at Durham University that I began to worry about what use I would be to the world at large with the ability to write Latin verse, a stunning in-depth knowledge of the Battle of Thermopylae, and an over-enthusiasm for Socratic argument

- a capability that, as my wife will inform you with heavy sighs, continues to deny me the will to agree with anybody about anything (naturally, I think she's wrong). The final nail in the coffin of my time with the Classics came with the querulous "Who are you?" of Professor Woodcock, whose lectures I had studiously avoided for over two years because of their stultifying boredom and who had kindly offered to explain the reasons for my third-class degree. From that day to this, I have never read another word of Greek or Latin.

Those of you with sharp geographical brains will have realised by now that, in attending Durham University, I was within spitting distance of the Roman Empire's greatest monument to its presence in Britain – Hadrian's Wall, which stretches from coast to coast across the north of England. It was built, as I knew well, to keep out the Scots barbarians who were actually, on my mother's side, my ancestors. And yes, we were given opportunities to visit, to excavate, to study, to marvel, et cetera, but somehow I became seduced by the more pressing glories of Newcastle Brown Ale, gambling on horses, and sex. By comparison with these, Hadrian and his monument paled and I never went near it. At the end of my time at Durham, I returned to Wolverhampton where there was still no call for Latin-speakers but there was a desperate shortage of English teachers, which is how I found employment.

But there's been something lurking at the back of my mind for the past 40 years, some unfinished business you might call it, I suppose. And the opening of the new Hadrian's Wall Path in 2003 seemed to call me into action to revisit some of my past in order to make some sense of it. Walking this new long-distance path provided me with the ideal opportunity to do just that.

Any fule kno, as Nigel Molesworth, the hero of that other famous product of 1953, Geoffrey Willans's wonderfully anarchic *Down with Skool*, might say, that Julius Caesar first invaded Britain in 55

B.C. Caesar had by this time divided Gaul into three parts but, although he was known as Julius Caesar the Roman Geezer, he had yet to become Emperor and had obviously yet to be stabbed by Brutus, falling dramatically to the ground in the Senate as he cried out those immortal words *"Et tu, Brute"*. The experts are still arguing about Caesar's reasons for invading Britain but what is most likely is that he'd heard about pork scratchings and wanted to find their source. Unfortunately, he timed his conquest badly and was forced to withdraw back across the sea to France until the following fighting season of 54 B.C., when he returned and got the British tribes of the south-east to submit. Then he uttered his immortal words *"Veni, vidi, vici"*, or "I came, I saw, I ate some pork scratchings". His fellow-countrymen back in Rome were mightily impressed that Julius had managed to cross the sea twice and come back each time. In fact, they were so impressed that a bit later they made him Emperor.

That was it for another 100 years, until the Emperor Claudius (dressed in a white toga and sounding remarkably like the stuttering Derek Jacobi) decided he needed to prove to his fellow citizens that he was a real hard knock too, even though he was a lily-livered coward at heart. So in A.D. 43 four of the famous Roman legions, commanded by Aulus Plautius, were put on the ro-ro ferry at Boulogne and set sail for Britain. On landing these 40,000 soldiers overwhelmed the local Kent hop-pickers and marched on Colchester, the home of the East End wide boys, who at that time were not much cop and were also rapidly overcome. Claudius then turned up with some elephants (he was always a bit of a show-off) and rode on a chariot in triumph through the town, accompanied by his wife Messalina and the generals who had done the real fighting. Within a few weeks, all the local kings of the south and east of England had submitted and Claudius thought he was the bees' knees of soldiering.

The Roman army was here to stay this time and it was another 400 years before it left. During that time the legions gradually spread westwards and northwards, driving the native Britons into

Wales and Cornwall and pushing the other Celtic tribes back into Scotland. What did the Romans want in Britain, apart from pork scratchings that is? Well, they were stuck with this daft belief that it was their mission to conquer the world and they just couldn't stop. Once the army was on the march, it had to keep on duffing up the barbarians wherever they were and however nice they really were when you got to know them. We'll come later to some of the truths and some of the myths about the Roman army but I'm pretty sure no-one will disagree with the fact that it was the finest fighting machine ever devised. The trouble with fighting machines, of course, is that they have to keep fighting to feel any purpose in life, and for a long time the Roman citizens were not very impressed with any Emperor who couldn't get the army into some kind of a punch-up and win.

The Romans also mined for gold, silver and other metals in Britain and used the extensive British countryside to produce large quantities of grain. In return for this, they built long straight roads, introduced the Britons to public baths and underfloor heating, and planted the first apples and pears, as well as most of the herbs that we now take for granted as part of our cuisine. All well and good, you might say, but was it worth coming all that way just for that? And the answer is that it almost certainly was not, but the problem with the Roman Empire, as I've already indicated, was that it was based on the Roman army, which just had to keep on going and going and going.

In A.D. 411 the Roman army eventually got fed up and withdrew from Britain. After that Latin was rarely spoken for a good six centuries, except by holy rollers in the monasteries and churches. It hung around a bit, of course, leaving its quaint sounds in the names of some of our towns and cities – London, for instance, and anything with *–castle* or *–caster* in it, but in general the later settlers of our island coming over from the continental mainland didn't bother with Latin and the previously-existing settlers, the original Brits, never really got far beyond *amo, amas, amat.*

Then came the Renaissance and suddenly everybody wanted to know how to conjugate *amo*, so grammar schools were founded to teach good old Latin prose and suddenly the island was awash with people spouting bits of dog Latin as if they were natives of Perugia or Florence. And this pre-eminence of Latin lasted nearly as long as the Roman army had stayed in Britain beforehand. Much of the schooling that I had was based on the requirement of universities right up to the 1960s for all upcoming students to have passed 'O' Level Latin. So everyone, even those who aspired merely to become bank managers or captains of local industry or Grand Viziers in the local Masonic Lodges, had to undergo training in this dead and obsolete language. Even in Wolverhampton! And that was what the Reverend Frank Rust launched me and my compatriots into that first September day back in 1953.

And that's how, indirectly and eventually, I came to walk the Roman Wall with the Emperor Hadrian.

Hadrian arrived in Britain in A.D. 122 for what a Roman poet called "a stroll among the Britons". But, as well as strolling, he had serious things on his mind which require me to give you a bit of background about the Romans in Britain between the time of Claudius's initial conquest and the building of the famous Wall.

Three names stand out in these 80 years, two Brits and one Roman. The Brits were Caractacus and Boadicea, who some years ago it became politically correct to refer to as Boudicca for some unknown reason. The Roman was Agricola, who, contrary to what many believe from the sound of his name, did not introduce Coca Cola to the country but rather advanced the Roman army further and further north. Let's spend a moment with each of these characters.

Caractacus first of all then. He and his brother Togodumnus, the sons of Cunobelinus, ruled southern England at the time of the invasion by Claudius's troops. Despite being forced back into the heartlands of Britain by the encroaching Roman army and its superior weaponry, Caractacus's men fought bravely until they decided on a final stand somewhere in the borders of what is now Wales. Here Caracatacus encouraged his men and told them that the work of that day would be the beginning of a new liberty or of eternal slavery. Even though he lost, his words seem to have haunted British leaders ever since. They are not unlike the sorts of appeal that Churchill made during the Blitz and they are uncomfortably similar to the sort of claptrap spouted by the British National Party to this day. Caractacus, however, was captured and paraded through the streets of Rome, so he's not a spectacularly good model to follow.

Next up is Boadicea, as I shall continue to call her, the original warrior queen that we still hark back to periodically in our national archetypes - think of Good Queen Bess and the thrashing of the Spanish Armada or Maggie Thatcher and her triumphant recovery of the Falklands. Boadicea was left a widow by the East Anglian king of the Iceni tribe. The Romans, thinking that the Iceni lands were now ripe for the taking, took an away-day to Norfolk, flogged Boadicea, raped her two daughters and planted their standard. Boadicea, being a ginger-haired Brit full of fire in her belly, was enraged by this treatment and led an army against the Roman towns of London, Colchester and St. Albans. As I recall it from my in-depth study of legend, she was a bit of a muscular wench who fought in a chariot, urging her soldiers on with her shield and trident. Or was that Britannia? Whatever, it seemed like a good idea at the time but the Roman army was a mean fighting machine and it pretty soon regrouped under the leadership of the governor Suetonius Paulinus and gave the Iceni a whacking. Boadicea, sensing the inevitable defeat, took poison and died. Rumour has it that she was buried under what is now Platform 8 of King's Cross Station!

And so to the only Roman in this saga, Agricola, who was governor of the province from A.D. 77 to 83 and whose story is told us by the Roman historian Tacitus (or "the silent we", as in bath), the governor's son-in-law, so he might be just a teeny bit biased. Agricola's first decision was to sort out the rebellious Taffs in north Wales which he did pretty quickly, despite being faced with black-robed women with hippy hairstyles and screeching Druids in white sheets. Tacitus throws an interesting light on his father-in-law's methods – a light that U.S. generals overseas might benefit from observing:

> *Agricola, however, understood the feelings of the province and had learned from the experience of others that arms can effect little if injustice follows in their train. Beginning with himself and his staff, he enforced discipline in his own establishment first – a task often found as difficult as the government of a province.*

Having imposed this discipline, he then started introducing the native Brits to civilization, providing a posh education for the sons of the chieftains (yes, it's still going on), building new public squares and houses, and encouraging the smelly locals to have baths. He even got them to ponce around in togas and to speak a sort of pidgin Latin.

Agricola's next step was to push the boundary further and further north, duffing up the local tribes on the way, and eventually into Caledonia reaching as far as the Tay estuary, where he planned to build a bridge. But then, in a moment of Nostradamian forethought, he paused and heard in the breeze the opening words of William McGonagall's great epic *The Tay Bridge Disaster*:

> *Beautiful Railway Bridge of the Silv'ry Tay!*
> *Alas! I am very sorry to say*
> *That ninety lives have been taken away*
> *On the last Sabbath day of 1879,*
> *Which will be remember'd for a very long time.*

Well, you would pause, wouldn't you? And you would think about that dreadful disaster that was yet to happen but which could have been prevented, according to the Scots bard, by buttresses. And you would wish you were back in Rome, watching the chariot racing or eating pork scratchings or anything that didn't require you to think about William McGonagall.

But next season – yes, there was an official duffing-up season in those days, coinciding with the better weather and allowing for the transfer of crack troops from the continent in the winter to strengthen the squad – Agricola set off to conquer the furthest reaches of northern Britain, the Scottish highlands. Here he engaged the Caledonians in the fierce Battle of Mons Graupius, nowadays known as Bennachie near Inverurie in Aberdeenshire.

This was a crucial encounter. 30,000 Jocks faced a Roman army of about 10,000, which was tightly disciplined and experienced in combat. Their front line was made up of auxiliaries from Holland and Belgium, with the Roman legionaries in the rear. Brutal hand-to-hand fighting took place. At one stage the Caledonians tried a sneaky move to outflank the Romans only to meet hidden Roman cavalry suddenly closing on them. That was the beginning of the end for them, as the superior Roman army pressed onwards. In a merciless bloodbath 10,000 Jocks were slaughtered. The following day according to Tacitus:

An awful silence reigned on every hand; the hills were deserted, houses smoking in the distance, and our scouts did not meet a soul.

You'd have thought that the sensible thing to do now was for Agricola to march on to conquer the rest of the Highlands but no, he was recalled to Rome, technically to have a parade in his honour but this effectively ended the northern conquest of Britain. Troubles elsewhere in Europe also led to the recall of one of the four legions stationed in Britain at the time and the troops gradually withdrew to the new border between the

River Tyne and the Solway Firth. Forts at Carlisle and Corbridge, already built to protect the supply lines on the south-to-north roads, were reinforced and the road that came to be known as the Stanegate was built to connect east to west.

And that was pretty much the scene when the Emperor Publius Aelius Hadrianus, to give him his proper name, or Hadrian as we all affectionately remember him, arrived on these shores.

Who was he, this new Emperor? That's what a lot of native Brits must have wondered at the time. And I became curious about him in reading about the Wall because he is notable for being largely invisible in most accounts. And that's why I decided that my account would tell of Hadrian as well as of his Wall.

For a start Hadrian was not the standard issue Roman Emperor, either in looks or in style or in strategy. He was the first Emperor to sport a beard, an affectation that he had picked up from his travels in Greece. Indeed he was so fond of the Greeks that he himself was known as Graeculus – the Greekling. His 16-year reign was unusual because he spent at least half of it away from Rome, inspecting the troops at the furthest outposts of the empire and ensuring that good discipline prevailed, as well as indulging his own passion for tourism. At the same time, Hadrian was the first Emperor to put limits to the Roman Empire, building earth or stone walls in north Africa and wooden palisades in Germany and, of course, erecting in Britain the Wall that was to bear his name for ever after. This was a significant step, because the whole purpose of the Roman Empire up till then had been to get bigger and bigger – to create an "empire without boundaries", as the Roman poet Virgil called it.

Hadrian was born on 24th January A.D. 76, which makes him an Aquarian and therefore one of the know-alls of the zodiac and someone who is original, inventive and very smart. Hadrian's family hailed from Italica, the Roman town close to Seville in Spain where sick and wounded soldiers from campaigns in North Africa had settled nearly 300 years earlier. Italica was also the home town of Hadrian's predecessor Trajan, which might give a clue why the former was adopted by the latter on the death of Hadrian's father in A.D. 85.

Hadrian's childhood and adolescence were spent in ways common to the kids of wealthy Romans. He had some exclusive schooling, he visited the family olive groves in Italica, he went hunting, he studied law, and he became an officer in the Roman army, serving in modern-day Hungary, Macedonia and Germany. In A.D. 98 Trajan was anointed as the new Emperor and a year later Hadrian married Sabina, who just happened to be the grandniece of the new Emperor. Smart move, eh? The next few years saw him rising through the ranks until in A.D. 117 Trajan officially adopted him as his heir – very timely because within a few months Trajan was dead and Hadrian became Il Padrone, The Boss, The Roman Geezer, the Capo di Capi.

So what do you do when you are suddenly thrust into this position? First of all, you set about ensuring stability, which may mean relegating, removing or otherwise disposing of your enemies. Hadrian was no different from any latter-day *mafioso* boss in this; he quickly but cleverly arranged for four of his arch-enemies in the Roman senate to be sent to sleep with the fishes, all while doing what a Roman's gotta do and marching with the troops in Syria, so he could deny responsibility. When he finally returned to Rome a year later, he initiated that other stock-in-trade for incoming leaders – a booze-up for the boys. In this case it was officially a gladiatorial show in the Colosseum in memory of Trajan but this was just Hadrian's way of letting the Romans enjoy a bit of a knees-up and reminding them to be grateful to the one who made it possible.

It was another three years before Hadrian reached Britain, having stopped off in Germany en route, where he ordered a wooden palisade to be built with huge oak posts split through the middle to mark the north-eastern boundary of the Empire. At the same time he tightened up the discipline in the troops, camping outdoors among the squaddies and sharing their basic diet of German sausage, sauerkraut and Liebfraumilch. This was an Emperor who realised that the best way to get the support of his army was to lead by example, living simply, marching with the troops rather than following in a chariot, and then demanding strict discipline from those amongst whom he had marched and camped.

In A.D. 122 Hadrian ordered the VI Victrix legion to Britain from Lower Germany and appointed its commander Platorius Nepos – an old buddy of the Emperor's from way back – as the new governor of the province. It seems likely that Hadrian himself arrived about the same time, probably with his wife Sabina and his secretary Suetonius, the Roman historian. However, these two were left in London with much of the imperial retinue and it was here that Suet Pudding disgraced himself by attempting a bit of hanky-panky with the Empress. It wasn't long before he was sent packing back to Rome and an inglorious career as a writer of Latin bodice-rippers such as *On Famous Whores*. Hadrian meanwhile had set off north to inspect the troops at the edge of the Empire and it was here and now that he ordered the building of his famous Wall.

The story goes that the VI Victrix legion sailed up the east coast of Britain to the River Tyne, where they dedicated two altars and set about building the Pons Aelius in the Emperor's memory where modern-day Newcastle is. Shortly afterwards, work on the Roman Wall commenced, preceded by Hadrian himself who went for his "stroll among the Britons" tracing the proposed line of the Wall from Wallsend to Bowness-on-Solway.

And, in the summer of 2004, I set out to follow in his footsteps.

I

STARTING IN SEGEDUNUM

*"Perhaps, I am the first man that ever travelled the
whole length of this Wall, and probably the last that
will attempt it."*

William Hutton, who wrote these words in 1802, could not have
been more wrong, though I doubt if anyone since has completed
the epic trek that he undertook. Aged 78, Hutton walked from
his home town of Birmingham to Carlisle in the summer of 1801,
traversed Hadrian's Wall to Wallsend, then returned along its
length to Bowness, before finally walking back to Birmingham.
It was a distance of over 600 miles. It was a prodigious feat (and
he must have had prodigious feet). The record he left us of his
journey is fascinating, entertaining and enlightening. However,
although Hutton was probably the first person since the Romans
to actually walk the length of the Wall, he was not the first to visit
it. Elizabeth I's historian, William Camden, was there and other
noteworthy antiquarians paid calls over the centuries. Since the
opening of the Hadrian's Wall Path in 2003, it is estimated that
several thousand people have walked the Wall and thousands
more will enjoy its delights in coming years. Some will start in the
west, on the atmospheric Solway Firth, and others will start, like I
did, in the east, in the place whose name forever bears the mark
of Hadrian's monument – Wallsend.

I was sitting in the Flavia Café at Segedunum, debating with
myself whether to sample peacock brains, pike livers, cock crests
or lark tongues, all of which were mentioned on the menu. In
the end, however, I stuck with the cheese sandwich and cup
of coffee I'd already decided on in preference to these Roman
delicacies. The Flavia Café is on an upper floor of the rather

wonderful Segedunum Roman fort, baths and museum complex in Wallsend, where my walk with Hadrian was to begin. In truth the café sells standard modern British fare but its menu tells you some interesting facts about Roman culinary habits, such as:

- The most commonly used spice in Roman times was pepper. The Romans used it to flavour game birds, fish, shellfish, lamb, kid and wild boar.
- There was a famous Roman food writer called Apicius - the equivalent of Ainsley Harriott or Jamie Oliver perhaps.
- Rich Romans would eat complicated dishes. One such dish involved stuffing a chicken inside a duck, then inside a goose, then inside a pig, then inside a cow and then cooking the whole lot together.
- A fish sauce and fish pickle were popular in Roman times, where the gills, blood and intestines of a mackerel were placed in a jar with salt, vinegar and herbs, pounded and stirred, then left to ferment in the sun.
- The Romans never discovered the secret recipe for pork scratchings.

After reading all that, I nearly choked on my cheese sandwich. But I have to say it does get you in the mood for the exploration of Segedunum and the start of all things Roman.

I'd caught a train to Newcastle and then travelled by metro to Wallsend, where I was rather tickled by the metro map with its Latin place names and its *Noli Fumare* (No Smoking) instruction. Then it was a short walk to Segedunum site, in the shadows of the Swan Hunter shipyard. The site was, until only 30 or so years ago, completely built over with terraced housing where the shipyard workers lived, but when that housing was demolished prior to redevelopment, excavations showed that the remains of the whole Segedunum fort were better preserved than had once been thought. In 2000 the Segedunum museum was finally opened and it is a truly wonderful experience to visit.

One of the highlights is the splendid vista of the laid out fort from the Viewing Tower. From outside, this tower looks like some kind of spaceship placed incongruously among these Roman relics but it is a most imaginative way of displaying the size and extent of the playing-card fort that the Romans exported across the globe. If you're hooked on this sort of thing, you'll be interested to note the signs of the barracks blocks, of the *horrea* (granary), of the *principia* building (headquarters), and of the *praetorium* (commanding officer's house).

After that I went to the reconstructed bath-house, built to the design of the surviving bath-house at Chesters fort on the Wall itself. Following the horde of primary school children being given their live lesson on "The Romans", I slipped off my jacket in the *apodyterium* (changing room), hugged myself in the *frigidarium* (cold room) with its pretty fish frescoes and its statue of Fortuna, the goddess of good luck, unbuttoned my shirt in the *tepidarium* (warm room), then stripped off completely in the *caldarium* (hot room). In this latter - a sort of Turkish Bath - a bevy of naked Geordie slave-girls used wooden strigils to scrape away my sweat, dirt and oil, all the time smiling lasciviously at me. Sorry, that was just a little bit of my febrile imagination, but you can tell I was really entering the spirit of the place, can't you? Finally it was into the *laconicium* (hot dry room) whose sauna-style heat finished off my bathing experience and left me fit for a night out in Wallsend. But more of that later.

Then it was back into the museum with all its up-to-the-minute gadgetry - touchy-feely video screens that show the history of the Segedunum site, from prehistory through Roman times to the collieries and shipbuilding of more recent days. I loved the audio-visual display where actors suitably toga'd or armoured tell of their daily lives in the fort, all in authentic Geordie-Roman accents. There's a neat model of the fort and a reconstruction of squaddies' rooms in a barracks block. There's also a lot of artefacts found during the excavations, all of which begin to get you in the mood for the start of the walk along the Wall. I found myself automatically remembering that the Romans always wrote in capital letters, that V equals 5, and that Latin is a bloody funny language.

My thirst for all things Roman unquenched, I headed back to Newcastle on the metro (being careful to observe *Noli Fumare*, of course) to see the splendid Roman bits in the Museum of Antiquities within the university site. This houses many of the early findings from excavations on the Wall when our Victorian forefathers thought of museums as places like zoos, where the extravagant and the rare should be kept under lock and key for our scrutiny. Nowadays, of course, we prefer to keep things on the sites where they were unearthed and seek to show, as at Segedunum, how these historic remnants might fit into the jigsaw of our understanding of history. Still, there are some remarkable chunks of masonry in the Museum of Antiquities that bring to life some of the people who built the Wall.

For instance, there's an orangey-brown altar, almost intact, which stands close to the main entrance and which was found in the River Tyne at Newcastle, somewhere close to where the Pons Aelius was believed to have spanned the river. The altar bears an inscription showing that it was dedicated to the god Neptune by the VI Victrix legion. Remember them? Ordered over from Germany by Hadrian under the command of his old pal Platorius Nepos to sail up the east coast of Britain and to build the first bridge across the Tyne, the eponymous Pons Aelius, ready for the Emperor's arrival to start his Wall? Staring at this altar suddenly began to bring these guys to light. What must they have thought, thousands of miles from home, having sailed up the treacherous North Sea and been set the task of building this bridge across the Tyne? I imagine the dedication to Neptune, god of the seas, would have been some kind of thanksgiving for having got there at all. But what did they make of this strange inhospitable land, full of Andy Capps quaffing Newcastle Brown, smoking Woodbines and speaking a strange Geordie dialect? I can only guess.

There's another altar stone with an inscription showing it was raised by the Fourth Cohort of Lingones (just popped over from Eastern France and lingering longer than they'd originally intended), which was one of the auxiliary forces stationed for quite some time at Segedunum. Then there are two pieces of masonry which contain inscriptions from the II Augusta legion, from Caerleon in South Wales to help with the Wall building. These are not from Newcastle but from different points on the Wall but again they were inscribed, as the text makes clear, during Hadrian's reign. One is even more specific, stating that it was created during the governorship of Aulus Platorius Nepos, who we know was in charge of Britain from A.D.122 to 125, so these squaddies from the south Wales garrison must still have been building the Wall in A.D. 125.

There's a lot of other good stuff in the museum, including a mock-up of the temple to the Persian god Mithras, commonly known of course as a Mithraeum. The cult of Mithras became very popular in the Roman army, which is strange since they had plenty of gods of their own to worship. Mithras is always portrayed with his twin torchbearers, Cautes and Cautopates, the former holding an uplifted torch whilst the latter has a down-turned torch. In this reconstruction the two of them are duly recreated in model form but, to tell the truth, they look more like gnomes from some Garden Centre. At any rate they failed to convince me of the need for due reverence. I'm sure this Mithraeum is a very accurate reproduction and that its deliberate gloominess replicates what such a temple would have looked and felt like but I could barely make out anything, so I returned to the main body of the museum instead.

Here my eyes lit upon some coins from Roman times and, in particular, on a *sestertius* bearing the head of Hadrian himself and dated A.D. 132-134 Some poor squaddie had dropped this in the River Tyne nearly 1900 years ago. What might he have purchased with that coin? A glass or two of wine, maybe? An hour with a Geordie prostitute? A ticket for a gladiatorial contest? Or a pirated copy of Viz?

I used modern cash to purchase my metro ticket back to Wallsend.

The Imperial Guest House where I stayed my first night is a little treasure in a grim Wallsend. When you arrive at the front door, you think it's just another terraced house in a row of similar and unprepossessing dwellings. But then you step inside and you're immediately in another world - a world of mahogany and velvet, of pre-Raphaelite prints, of candelabras on mantelpieces, of gentle lighting and of Victorian opulence. The Imperial's owner, Colin Brownlee, has created this jewel with affection and care. Not only are the décor and the ambience extravagant and luxurious but the fare on offer is also. The ingredients of the full English breakfast are all sourced from Northumbria and a range of Twinings teas is available, as well as exclusively blended coffee.

For my overnight stay I was given the Collingwood suite, named after Admiral Lord Collingwood, the Geordie naval commander who took over the fleet on Nelson's death at the Battle of Trafalgar and whose picture adorned the wall of the bedroom. The canopied bed looked inviting but first I needed to eat and so, on Colin's advice, I headed for The Anson in the centre of Wallsend. This pub, named after a battleship made at Swan Hunter shipyard, stands on the site of an old pub called the Penny Wet and is at the heart of Wallsend.

Now this was Friday night but I was unprepared for the volume of people and of noise as I entered The Anson at about seven thirty in the evening. There were about six TV screens, mounted high towards the ceiling, all showing a rugby league match, though you couldn't hear the commentary because there was also a DJ playing extremely loud music and shouting at the hordes, plus I swear that there was a juke box playing somewhere. The place was choc-a-bloc with Geordie lasses in short skirts (blue denim seemed to be *de rigeur* that night), white stilettos, full make-up and cheap scent, either sitting with or eying up groups of Geordie lads in vests, tattoos and sunburnt faces, looking as if they'd just finished building the Wall that afternoon. In fact the longer I stayed there, the more I began to fantasise that these folk were the equivalent of the soldiers and civilians that might have met up on a Friday night way back when Segedunum was occupied by the Roman forces.

I ordered fish and chips, and as I waited for them to arrive, I watched trays of foaming beer and plates of food being juggled through the crowds. Next to me was a grossly-overweight couple who barely spoke to each other all the time I was there. Across the room a young bloke with a ready smile was chatting up three girls who tittered appropriately at his words and indulged in a bit of eyelid fluttering. A sudden gust from the opened door ushered in a group of eight young shaven-headed lads, clearly under age. The barman, however, quickly spotted them and, even when they sent the oldest-looking of them to order drinks, he refused to be fooled.

Celebrating the end of the week. The Nervians and the Lingones, both from eastern France, who we know were stationed at Segedunum at various times, might well have observed similar rituals, popping down to a *taverna* in the local civilian settlement that grew up around the fort itself. Their drug of choice would also probably have been beer; the local lasses would have been attracted by soldiers with money and uniforms, as they are everywhere; the local lads would have resented them and Friday night punch-ups would have occurred. Chariot-racing on the TV? Cithara-playing on the juke-box? Not yet, perhaps, but the soldiers would have had their favourite songs and we know that the fame of certain gladiators spread across the Roman Empire like wildfire.

Back at the Imperial, I did as Colin Brownlee had instructed and had a few moments in the opulent first-floor lounge, where a notice urges you to have a complimentary glass of port or sherry.

7

Bet the Nervians and the Lingones never had that! I poured myself a port.

"You look mighty pleased with yourself," said the glass of port.

"Thank you for the compliment," I replied, sipping in as refined a manner as I could.

Climbing into bed that night, I felt I had already begun my journey through time. Wallsend may be a grim place nowadays but that evening in The Anson had begun to transport me back through history and remind me of the timelessness of human life.

II

HADRIAN THE BRICKIE

Now, naturally, there's not a lot of point in being Emperor if you have to get your hands dirty doing menial jobs and, although Hadrian was not averse to doing a spot of wild camping or a stretch of route-marching *pour encourager les autres*, as the Gauls might have said, there was no way that he himself would have been involved in the building of the Wall that was to take his name. In fact, it's quite possible that he never saw any of it actually built but we do know that he had a great passion for architecture and it's likely that the original design of the Wall would have owed much to him. Some scholars speculate that an initial section of the Wall may have been built for Hadrian's inspection when he arrived at the frontier in A.D. 122 After all, the Roman army had in its midst enough skilled craftsmen to do this and very quickly, so it's not beyond the bounds of possibility.

Let's have a look at Hadrian's design for this barrier to keep out the barbarians. The Wall was planned to cross from Newcastle on the River Tyne to the Solway Firth, a total length of 80 Roman miles (74 English ones). It was to be built of stone for most of the way but of turf in the western sector where it is thought that there was no limestone to make mortar. It was to be ten feet wide and stand fourteen feet high. The method was that stone slabs were laid on puddled clay to form the foundations, on which was built the fourteen-foot wall of rubble faced with dressed stones, usually bonded with mortar. A reasonable guestimate for the amount of dressed facing stones on the finished Wall is 25 million – some work, eh? For some reason known only perhaps to Hadrian himself, the stone wall appears to have been completed with a coat of lime-wash plaster. The turf stretch of the Wall, unsurprisingly, consisted of turfs.

On the northern side of the Wall a huge ditch was to be dug, nine feet deep and thirty feet wide. Every Roman mile (remember, a little less than ours) a milecastle was to be built into the Wall with a watchtower or turret every third of a mile between each pair of milecastles.

So far, so good, but now the modifications kick in. At some unknown stage, the width of the Wall was reduced from ten feet to eight feet and this change began, for some curious reason, about 27 miles from the eastern beginning in Newcastle. At the same time the Wall was extended further east, using this new eight-feet width, to Wallsend, where my journey began. Then, again for some unknown reason, it was decided to build new forts on the line of the Wall, roughly every seven and a bit miles, and to dig another huge ditch, christened by the Venomous Bede as the Vallum, 30 feet to the south of the Wall.

The jury's still out on why these modifications were made, as it is on what the purpose of the Wall was. Those who, like me, learned Latin at school but who, unlike me, found opportunities to use such learning in their adult lives are still digging away and debating all these things. But what we can be reasonably sure of is that the Wall was substantially complete by A.D. 130, even though it was subsequently modified, and that the brickieing was carried out by members of three of the four legions then stationed in Britain – II Augusta from Caerleon in South Wales, XX Valeria Victrix from Chester and VI Victrix from York.

As for Hadrian, having launched the project on Tyneside, he went for his "stroll among the Brits" to survey the line of the Wall that was about to be built and then, before winter arrived in A.D. 122, he was off to Spain for a spot of late autumn sunbathing.

A lot of people think that the Romans were fairly boring for people who founded an empire. They don't have the magical allure of the Greeks, for example, with their philosophers strolling around spouting forth great truths, or their remarkable poets and playwrights, or their invention of that political system of democracy that we still think is the best way for people to manage their affairs (and why we periodically bomb some other country to smithereens to prove it). They don't have the mystery of the ancient Chinese empire, the intrigue of the Moghul Indian empire, nor the golden sheen of the Aztecs. But what the Romans did have was this incredible magpie-like capacity for stealing ideas from everywhere and applying them universally and to larger structures than had ever been dreamed of.

Just think of arches, for instance. Or, to be more precise, The Arch. Now the Egyptians, the Babylonians and the Greeks all knew about arches and used them, mostly in the building of underground drains. And the Assyrians actually used arches in their construction of an aqueduct to bring fresh water to the city of Nineveh. But nobody used the arch like the Romans did, principally to build bridges right across their empire so that every river was easily passable and the legions could march to any outpost of empire in as short a time as possible without getting their feet wet. You could walk, for example, if you were that way inclined, right the way from the English Channel to Rome without ever having to take off your sandals to ford a stream. Wow!

The arch was also at the heart of those huge and magnificent aqueducts that the Romans threw up across the empire to bring fresh water from long distances into the towns and cities of the peoples that they conquered. We can still see what these looked like in the remnants of the Pont du Gard in Nîmes and the aqueduct in Segovia, which is still used to carry water 2000 years after it was first constructed. So the conquered citizens, once they'd given up revolting, got fresh drinking water, which they'd never had, and discovered washing, which they'd mostly never bothered with previously (which was why, of course, they were revolting).

Hadrian was actually so in love with the idea of arches that later in his career in A.D. 131 he had a triumphal arch built on the road connecting the old city of Athens to the new bit (which he had had built, of course). The arch carried two inscriptions, one on either side: the first, on the side facing the Acropolis read, "This is Athens, the ancient city of Theseus"; the second, on the other side facing the new city read, "This is the city of Hadrian and not of Theseus". Modest or what?

The arch was also a constant feature in the public buildings that the Romans erected everywhere. Take the Pantheon in Rome itself, originally built at the time of the Emperor Augustus but significantly rebuilt at the time of and under the jurisdiction of the Emperor Hadrian himself, after it had twice previously been destroyed by fire – once when Nero was playing his fiddle. The Pantheon is still standing, nearly 2000 years after its first construction, which is a tribute to the engineering and architectural talents of Hadrian and his builders. It's taller from floor to ceiling than St. Peter's in the Vatican, it's a completely free-standing building, and it was the very first hemispherically domed structure ever successfully erected. At the centre of the dome, thus creating a flood of light inside the building, is a 27-foot-wide opening called an *oculus*. Every domed building subsequently created anywhere in the world owes its inspiration to Hadrian's marvellous Pantheon.

The Emperor Augustus boasted that he found Rome a city of brick and left it a city of marble. And the explosion in civic buildings begun in his time, using the newly-discovered quarries of northern Italy and borrowing from Greek architectural styles, is a fitting and apt tribute to his boast. But the big secret of Hadrian's reconstructed Pantheon was the use of concrete. Now, like so much else, the Romans did not invent concrete but what they did was develop it into a form that gave incredible strength and durability. The secret ingredient, discovered accidentally by a Roman apprentice with a hangover from drinking too much cheap Asti Spumanti, was a volcanic ash called *pozzolan*. This, when mixed with the sort of thin, white, burnt limestone, in use since Moses was a lad in the reeds, created a thick substance that dried into a strong bonding agent which, crucially, could be submerged in water and withstand it. Something similar is used nowadays to make dams in America and elsewhere. It is this firm-setting Roman concrete, coupled with incredible engineering and design skills, that has enabled the Pantheon to survive almost intact to this day.

The notion of a city was, of course, foreign to the British, as it had been to most of the peoples conquered by the Romans. What was the point? Not a lot, in their view, because they preferred wandering around and making camp wherever there was food or women or precious metals or whatever took their fancy. Cities were a waste of space, literally, as far as the ancient Brits were concerned. And they were not alone in thinking this. Virtually all of the major cities of France, Spain and Germany have Roman origins. The Roman architects and engineers found steady employment creating these cities, whose central features were the forum, the amphitheatre, and the public baths, all of which were designed, naturally, to demonstrate to the natives that the Romans were the bosses.

Let's start with the forum. A modern equivalent would be a combination of town hall, law court, marketplace and church all combined in a single structure. It was a novel notion to those Brits who gained Roman citizenship that you could go to this single building at the centre of town to get justice, pay your taxes, and do your weekly retail therapy. You were also able to publicly spout your opinions in the forum about hot topics such as asylum seekers or the price of pork scratchings and pass the time of day with your fellow citizens.

As far as amphitheatres go, there's not a lot of visible evidence in Britain; at least, there's nothing like the magnificent Colosseum in Rome. Though none of them have survived as well as some in Italy, there were 19 amphitheatres known to exist in Britain, including three attached to military forts. These were at Caerleon, Chester and York. Archaeologists recently discovered the outline of a further example in London, which measures about 100 by 85 metres and would have been able to seat around 6,000 people. By comparison the Colosseum in Rome would have been able to seat 50,000 people. The basic design of the amphitheatre was similar across the Roman Empire. Its arena was elliptical in shape and it had three tiers of seats all around it. Around its perimeter were a number of equally-sized entrance archways (yes, that arch again). In fact, all modern sports stadia, including Wembley and Cardiff's Millennium Stadium (and Molineux Stadium, the home of the wonderful Woverhampton Wanderers), as you have no doubt recognised, are built to the same principles. Clever stuff, eh?

Then there were the public baths. Regular washing and bathing as practised by the Romans would certainly have been a strange notion to the smelly Brits watching the building of public baths everywhere, including at each fort on the Wall. The first secret was, of course, in bringing a supply of water into the city by means of the aqueducts that the Roman engineers became so skilful in building. The second secret was in the invention of underfloor heating by pipes, or hypocausts as the Romans called them. With these two magic ingredients, the Roman engineers could provide the facilities which would enable their citizens to wash regularly and also to indulge themselves in sport and gossip.

Remember, these bath houses were not quiet places where you could expect to lie on your back in the water and contemplate the universe or your navel. No, the Roman writer Seneca, writing some 60 years before Hadrian came to Britain, describes a typical bath house thus:

> *"Here I am with a babel of noise going on all about me. I have lodgings right over a public bath-house. Now imagine to yourself every kind of sound that can make one weary of one's years. When the strenuous types are doing their exercises, swinging weight-laden*

hands about, I hear the grunting as they toil away – or go through the motions of toiling away – at them, and the hissings and strident gasps every time they expel their pent up breath. When my attention turns to a less active fellow who is contenting himself with an ordinary inexpensive massage, I hear the smack of a hand pummelling his shoulders, the sound varying as it comes down flat or cupped. But if on top of this some ball player comes along and starts shouting out the score, that's the end! Then add someone starting up a brawl, and someone else caught thieving, and the man who likes the sound of his own voice in the bath, and the people who leap into the pool with a tremendous splash."

It makes my local swimming baths with its large lads bombing seem rather dull by comparison.

Hadrian himself often bathed in the public baths, even with the common crowd, and there's an amusing tale told of him:

"For on a certain occasion, seeing a veteran, whom he had known in the service, rubbing his back and the rest of his body against the wall, he asked him why he had the marble rub him, and when the man replied that it was because he did not own a slave, he presented him with some slaves and the cost of their maintenance. But another time, when he saw a number of old men rubbing themselves against the wall for the purpose of arousing the generosity of the Emperor, he ordered them to be called out and then to rub one another in turn."

Apparently, this jest made Hadrian famous. I suppose it's the way you tell 'em, but this drollery does not make me weep with laughter, though I suppose it might have gone down well in Upper (and Lower) Germany.

The most famous baths in Britain were, appropriately enough, at Bath, though the Romans referred to the place as Aquae Sulis. Here they discovered hot water gushing out of a deep spring at a temperature of 46 Celsius and at a rate of 240,000 gallons every day, which must have seemed like very heaven in this cold northern island they had conquered and now had to live in. It's difficult to date the founding of Aquae Sulis because there have been so many modifications to it over the centuries but the huge curative baths the Romans built there were the largest of their kind in western Europe. It appears that the original plan was for three swimming baths in a series with the Great Bath being the last one. At some stage the Great Bath was roofed over by a great tunnel vault that was 35 feet across.

Today the Roman Baths still stand at Bath but, until you manage to get there, you can make do temporarily with some Aquae Sulis facial scrub, toner, moisturiser, or facial oil from a company that makes such products, using water from the nearby Mendip Hills. I don't know if Hadrian tried any of these products, maybe to keep his skin looking soft and lovely, but it's quite possible he called in at Aquae Sulis for a quick scrub during his visit to Britain. Tacitus would only have heard of Aquae Sulis from his father-in-law Agricola – a pity really because the Great Bath would have been perfect for the Silent We.

Now we can't discuss Roman building without some reference to that other major memento to their time in charge of the world and that is, of course, the famously straight Roman roads. It is estimated that during their 400 years or so in Britain the Romans built over 10,000 miles of roads. Many of them are still in use to-day, some of them household names like Watling Street, the Fosse Way, Dere Street or Ermine Street. And the same is true across Europe wherever the Roman Empire reached.

Watling Street was the first road to be built in Britain, or at least the initial stretch of it that ran from Richborough, where the

Roman fleet first landed with Aulus Plautius and his legionaries, to Canterbury and then onwards towards London, as the troops continued their conquest of Kent. By the time that the Emperor Claudius with his elephants was ready to arrive, the Roman road engineers had built a huge new road from London to Colchester as well. As the conquest of Britain continued over the following years, so the road network expanded. When Agricola turned up to take over as governor, there was already a substantial road network linking London to the north as far as York. Agricola's troops were responsible for driving two new routes north of York, Le Street to the east going via Chester-le-Street to Newcastle and onwards along the line of the modern A1, and Dere Street to the west leading via Catterick to Corbridge and onwards into Scotland. It is believed that the Stanegate, connecting the Roman forts at Stanwix/Carlisle and Corbridge, was built in this same period.

We don't know if any new roads were built for Hadrian's visit to Britain, though it is almost certain that there would have been squads of legionaries wearing donkey jackets and yellow hard hats patching up the existing thoroughfares. It may be that all these northern roads were repaired for Hadrian's arrival in Britain, so that his entourage could travel smoothly on their northern jaunt.

It's not true, by the way, that the Romans built straight roads in order to stop their soldiers going round the bend (or to stop the Britons hiding round the corner). The main purpose in building these roads was to enable the Roman troops, marching on foot, to get from A to B as quickly as possible and to allow the supplies to be brought up behind them with equal promptness. That's why they run in straight lines, as far as possible. For, unlike the Brits they found on the island who had made do for thousands of years with gentle ambles around the hillsides to exercise their dogs, the Romans were not bothered about gradients. It's true, as I know from my own walking experience, that once you're on the march it's actually easier to go straight over a hill than to skirt around the bottom of it. And the Roman army always wanted to get there fast, no matter where 'there' was or even if there was such a place.

The soldiers themselves built the roads, whose routes were laid out by surveyors who were also part of the army, using beacon fires and a tool called a *groma*. This latter, which looks like a badly-made hatstand, is the rather unwieldy predecessor of modern surveying tools, like you see spotty young men in yellow anoraks gazing through on roadsides from time to time. Once the line of the road was determined, the squaddies set to work, clearing the ground of rocks, trees and bushes, then digging a trench about three feet deep. Into this they placed a foundation layer of large stones, followed by a second layer of smaller stones, followed by a layer of gravel that was sometimes mixed with cement and broken tiles, then finally the top surface consisted of a layer of paving stones, cut to fit closely into each other. It's not unlike how McAlpine's Fusiliers build roads to this day, except that we now have a different top surface.

Roman roads could extend to 17 feet across but a feature of these roads has had a major influence on the subsequent development of transportation systems world-wide. Do you know why the standard distance between the rails on railways across the world is exactly four feet, eight and a half inches? No? Well, it's because the first railway on which George Stephenson's *Rocket* completed its trial run was built that way. Why? Because the railway lines were built by the same people who had built the tramways. And why were they like that? Because the people who built the tramways used the same tools they had used to build wagons, which had the same spacing between their wheels. "And why was that?" I hear you cry. Well, it was quite simply because the good old English roads were so rutted that the wagons would have broken up if they hadn't had wheels that fitted within the ruts. And what made those ruts in the first place? You've got it – the great Roman war chariots, made just wide enough to accommodate the back ends of two war-horses.

There's an amusing add-on to this story, which concerns the huge booster rockets attached to the main fuel tanks of American space shuttles. Apparently these booster rockets have to be transported by train from the factory where they're made to the launch sites. The trains have to go through a series of tunnels which are, of course, only slightly wider than the railroad track itself. So the major design feature of what is arguably the world's most advanced transportation system was determined by the width of a horse's backside!

III
HEADING FOR HEDDON

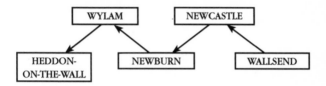

So, here I was then. I enjoyed my Imperial breakfast, graciously served by Colin himself, and set off to the beginning of the Hadrian's Wall Path beside Segedunum and in the shadows of the Swan Hunter shipyard with its massive red and yellow cranes hovering above me. Swan Hunter used to be synonymous with shipbuilding on the Tyne but, if I'd undertaken my journey some 20 years ago in the mid-1980s, I would have found that only four people worked there and they were security guards. Swan Hunter has been in existence for over 150 years. In its time it has produced some 1600 ships of varied types including more than 400 naval vessels. These include such famed vessels as the *Carpathia*, which rescued 700 survivors (but not Leonardo di Caprio) from the *Titanic* answering a distress call received 58 miles away, and the *Mauretania*, which was the largest passenger ship ever built on the Tyne and which for 20 years held the Blue Riband for the fastest Atlantic crossing from New York to Liverpool, achieved on its first voyage.

Shipbuilding was a casualty of the Thatcher years, when the Iron Lady's government set about privatising state-run industries, destroying the trades unions, and creating mass unemployment. It was no accident that Elvis Costello's angry cry against the Falklands War was entitled *Shipbuilding*, with its mournful refrain:

Within weeks they'll be re-opening the shipyards
And notifying the next of kin
Once again
It's all we're skilled in
We will be shipbuilding
With all the will in the world
Diving for dear life
When we could be diving for pearls.

I had been surprised the previous evening, as I left Segedunum, to see groups of workers leaving Swan Hunter's and had asked Colin Brownlee at breakfast what the current situation was.

"Yes, the shipbuilding's back now," he told me. "All thanks to that Dutchman."

"Who's that?" I asked.

"His name's Jaap Kroese. He used to work on the rigs and made his money in the North Sea. He rescued the yards."

"How come?"

"The management was useless," he told me angrily. "They could have saved the whole lot. Even right up to the time when they were waiting for the receivers, they could have saved the yard. They were offered a contract to build industrial boilers but they turned it down. Said they were shipbuilders, not boiler builders. They were stark staring bonkers."

"Then what happened?" I pressed, buttering a slice of toast.

"Then it closed down. Everyone lost their jobs," Colin told me. "But now they're taking on apprentices again. Business is booming. All thanks to that Dutchman."

Well, it's not quite as good as Colin told me. True, Jaap Kroese has rescued Swan Hunter and the company has won contracts from the Ministry of Defence to build ships but those orders run out in 2006 and Kroese is warning that he may have to mothball the yard if no more orders come in. Still, it's pretty impressive that he has done what he has done, bringing new hope to this economically depressed area. Long may he succeed.

Just inside the Segedunum site there's a neat piece of reconstructed Wall which bears the names of those soldiers who built the Wall and scratched their names on it somewhere. There exists seemingly an eternal need for humans to make their mark on the world. How could they have guessed that here, nearly 1900 years later, I, by making my marks on this page, would be honouring them? I paused to scan the list before heading off on the first stage of my journey on the Hadrian's Wall Path.

From Wallsend until well east of Newcastle, the Wall itself is invisible, buried under the teeming streets of the metropolis, some of its stone used over the centuries in the foundations of other buildings or simply transported elsewhere for construction of such places as Tynemouth Abbey. Setting off, I followed the line of an old railway track past banks of pink dog-roses, ox-eye daisies, startlingly yellow birds-eye trefoil, purple lupins and golden honeysuckle. Suddenly there was the salty smell of the sea, as the path bent downhill from the converted rail track and on to the banks of the River Tyne itself. I looked back in the direction of the sea and imagined the Roman navy's ships, with their banks of oars, sweeping upstream to carry the VI Victrix legion and its commander Aulus Platorius Nepos to Newcastle. How did they decide where to build the Pons Aelius? Had the land and river already been surveyed?

I pressed on alongside the river, past the odd fisherman and being passed by the even odder jogger in green spandex pants and silver headphones, until I reached St. Peter's marina. This is a relatively new development, full of posh boats and even posher apartment buildings, symbolic of the new wealth that is creeping into the north east. I saw from my map that the area just to the north of here is called Byker, which was the site chosen for the BBC children's TV drama *Byker Grove*, now in its tenth year. This programme was responsible for foisting on an unsuspecting world the TV presenters known as Ant and Dec, better known to tweenage linguists as Ant 'n' Dec. These two young actors get voted top celebrities and are extremely popular with modern yoof and modern yoof's mums, who see them as cute and cuddly. It wouldn't surprise me if Ant 'n' Dec didn't have luxury cruisers moored in St. Peter's marina - a far cry from the decrepit youth club in *Byker Grove* where they first made their names.

A short deviation from the riverside hereabouts brings you around the back of Spiller's Flour Mill, forever associated in my mind with Fred Flour, the bowler-hatted plastic model used as Spiller's advertising logo back in the 1970s. This mill was built by Spiller's in 1938 and in its day was the largest flour mill in Europe, storing some 34,000 tons of grain. Spiller's is now part of some great conglomerate and this particular mill now produces animal feed, not flour. Just across the river from here, on the Gateshead side, another former mill has been converted into the Baltic Arts complex or BALTIC, as its creators prefer it to be known. Built with several million pounds of Arts Council money from the National Lottery, the old mill building was converted in order to accommodate five galleries, artists' studios, a cinema/ lecture space, a media lab, a library and an archive for the study of contemporary art. Opened in 2002 BALTIC proclaims itself to be "a new breed of public art space, an Art Factory". The even grander Sage Concert Hall, designed by Norman Foster, was taking shape just down river.

I nipped across that other symbol of the new Newcastle, the Millennium Bridge, or the Blinking Eye Bridge as it's better known locally, to have a look at BALTIC and I found it absolutely splendid. Apart from the ever-changing displays and the sheer sense of space within the building, it has a wonderful rooftop restaurant with terrific views of the River Tyne itself, of Newcastle city and of the whole spread of Tyneside. Mind you, you're only allowed in there if you've made a reservation for dining. Feigning ignorance, I caught the lift up to it anyway and pretended to scrutinise the menu, even though my shorts and cagoule may have suggested I was not entirely serious about eating there. I could just about afford a bread roll and thought about purchasing one, just so I could throw the crusts out of the window on to some passers-by. Just for the hell of it. But I resisted. Instead, I shrugged my shoulders at the waiter and said I'd try something a little simpler and – surprise, surprise – he seemed grateful I was not staying.

This stretch of the walk takes in all the Newcastle bridges and each is helpfully described in signage along the quayside where trendy wine bars and cafés have opened up in recent years in place of the redundant dock buildings and factories. First to be passed under is the 1928 Tyne Bridge, the longest single-span bridge in Britain when it was built and on which the Sydney Harbour bridge was based. Next comes the Swing Bridge of 1876, built by the local entrepreneur William Armstrong who was a mighty force on Tyneside, as you will see shortly. This is the fifth bridge known to have existed on this site, the original almost certainly having been Hadrian's Pons Aelius.

Then there's the magnificent two-tiered High Level Bridge of 1849, which carries trains on its upper level and cars on its lower. This bridge was designed by George Stephenson's son Robert and so impressed Queen Victoria when she opened it that she agreed to open the Royal Border Bridge at Berwick a year later. Now aren't you impressed?

After that the royals couldn't keep away from Geordieland. The 1906 rail bridge was opened by King Edward VII; the 1981 Metro bridge was opened by our present Queen; and finally there's the 1983 Redheugh road bridge, which was opened by the late Princess Di of blessed memory.

Incidentally, Newcastle library gives four interesting explanations for the term Geordie. I'd always thought it owed its origins to the 1745 Jacobite Rebellion when Bonnie Prince Charlie and his kilted pals, with their sporrans and their lucky heather, marched south and bypassed Newcastle because it was believed that its inhabitants were supporters of George III. From this time the local inhabitants became known as Geordies. And that is certainly one possible explanation.

Another claim is that it owes its origins to the local pits, where many poems and songs refer to Geordies. No less a source than the *Oxford English Dictionary* states that the word has two meanings - a guinea, which had the figure of St. George on it, and a pitman, hence Geordies were coal-miners. Now everyone in the north east was a coal miner, weren't they? (think about "taking coals to Newcastle"), so they were all Geordies.

A third possible explanation is that the term owes its origins to George Stephenson, who not only invented the railway but also the miners' lamp in use in north east collieries. Hence miners became Geordies from their safety helmets.

The fourth and final version is also connected to George Stephenson who addressed a Parliamentary Commission on Railways where his broad dialect drew contemptuous sneers. From then on the keelmen, who transported coal from the Tyne to the Thames, were referred to by Londoners as Geordies.

This seems an appropriate moment to tell a Geordie story, delivered of course in a thick Geordie accent.

A Geordie lad came in from work one day and said to his father,

"Fethor, I'd like to get married."

"Oh aye!" says his father. "Who do you intend to marry?"

"Why!" says the lad. "Sadie Robson."

"Ye divvent mean Sadie Robson from Woodbine Terrace? Cos ye canna marry hor, son. Ye see, when I was a lad, I got aboot a bit, and that lass is yor sister and my dowter."

A fortnight later the lad approached his father again, with a view to getting married.

"Who is it this time?" says the old man.

"Jenny Simpson," says the lad.

"I told ye afore," says his father. "I got aboot when I was young. That lass is yor sister and my dowter."

When the young Geordie's mother came in from shopping, her son's sitting crying. When she asked him why, he told her the whole story, how twice his father had refused him and why.

"Take na heed of him son," she says. "He's not yor father, anyhoo."

Oh me lads ye shud a' seen us gannin'
Passin' the folks upon the road,
Just as they were stannin'.
Thor was lots o' lads and lasses there
All wi' smilin' faces
Gannin' alang the Scotswood Road
Te' see the Blaydon Races.

The big excitement of the morning for me was when the Hadrian's Wall Path veered away from the river side and on to the

Scotswood Road itself, where I passed no smiling faces but was nearly run over by several scowling faces behind the steering wheels of huge container trucks on what is now a major thoroughfare out of Newcastle. This area was where William Armstrong created the huge manufacturing estate which at its height covered 230 acres and had a workforce of over 20,000 people producing steel, ships, munitions and hydraulic equipment.

I've already mentioned the Swing Bridge that Armstrong built but he was also responsible for inventing the Armstrong gun, which was a huge field gun firing specially studded 150-pound shells for distances of up to five miles. This was introduced to the British army in 1859 but its big success was when it was used in the American Civil War. Armstrong was made Engineer to the War Department and knighted because of this gun. Having got a taste of international capitalism, Armstrong then proceeded to make naval destroyers for the Japanese fleet. *The Asama* and *The Leopard* were used in the Russo-Japanese Wars of 1904-05 and subsequently Admiral Togo paid a fleeting visit to Newcastle to say *Arigato gozaimasu* (go on, look it up – I had to).

As for the Blaydon Races, they began on Whit Monday in 1861, designed to entertain the workers of Newcastle on their traditional day off. The *Blaydon Races* song was written and sung by George Ridley, an ex-miner whose leg was crushed in a pit accident. He first performed it in 1862 at Balmbra's Royal Music Saloon and the song, with its local references and a chorus which lends itself to tuneless drunken bawling, became instantly popular. Balmbra's re-opened as a music hall in 1962, to celebrate the centenary of the Blaydon Races, but is now a public house. The Blaydon Road Race, following the course of the route along the Scotswood Road outlined in the song, is held annually and attracts top athletes from across the world, competing for the Newcastle Brown Ale cup, the Dutton Foreshaw Chainbridge Ladies trophy, the Me and Wor Lass trophy, and the Blaydon Bell Veterans trophy. Sadly, for I rather fancied my chances of winning the latter, I'd missed it by three days.

After gannin' along the Scotswood Road, I was ready for some refreshment and, where the route took me along the former Wylam Waggonway and into the district of Newburn, I took a slight detour to find The Keelman for my lunch stop. The Keelman, housed in a former water pumping station, is the home of the Big Lamp Brewery and I indulged myself with a couple of pints of Old Lamp to help the passage of the excellent beef and horseradish roll I purchased from the bar. It was a pleasant Saturday afternoon, so I sat outside with the other weekending Geordies, some with families, some just enjoying a quiet pint, and at the table next to mine a group of rowers bemoaning the low levels of water in the river because of the dryness of the spring. The talk was all of oars, rowlocks and bowlocks. I couldn't make sense of it at all but have to say it was probably appropriate to have boat talk in a pub called The Keelman. Which brought to mind another musical fragment:

Weel may the keel row,
The keel row, the keel row
Weel may the keel row
That my wee laddie's in.

This was one of those songs that we used to sing at primary school, in the days before boy bands became all the rage. The word keel is from the Anglo-Saxon word *ceol* for a ship. On the River Tyne it was applied to an oval, flat-bottomed boat used for carrying twenty tons of coal at a time from upriver to the coal ships in the harbour. The keelmen used a large oar at the stern to push the boat along, a bit like those used in punts. The keelmen were famous for their hard lives, drinking and knocking their wives around, which nobody told me at primary school.

Duly fortified, I headed back on to my path through the Riverside Country Park and followed the bank of the river for a very pleasant stretch. I was feeling distinctly mellow after those two pints, as I headed out of the city's suburbs and into the countryside. I whistled *The Blaydon Races* and then *The Keel Row* tunelessly, I suspect, but somehow the lightness of those tunes matched my mood.

The Wylam Waggonway, whose tracks I was striding along that afternoon, has a historic significance which it is hard to credit from its current tranquil setting. It was the site of one of the earliest attempts to use steam trains, namely *Puffing Billy* and *Wylam Dilly*, which were used to transport coal from the nearby Wylam colliery down to the river in Newcastle. Appropriately enough, these trains operated on a stretch of line that went past the birthplace of the greatest railway engineer, George Stephenson himself, whose famed *Locomotion* opened the Stockton & Darlington line in 1825 and whose even more famed *Rocket* opened the Liverpool & Manchester railway some five years later. The latter, as well as being famous in its own right, is also notorious for being the site of the world's first railway accident when the M.P. William Huskisson, who was there to celebrate the opening, was knocked down in a freak accident and died.

George Stephenson's birthplace is a short detour off the official path, continuing on the old Wylam Waggonway, so I decided to pay a brief visit.

"Are ye looking for a cup of tea mebbe?" was the greeting I received from the lady in a black dress and white mob cap sitting outside the modest cottage with her two younger companions.

Her name was Helen and she had such a smile on her face that I could not refuse but first I wanted the guided tour. It was only a quid and, when I say guided tour, you shouldn't come too full of expectation. This is a tiny cottage, after all, the sort of place where our forefathers brought up 26 children on twopence a week and were still very happy. It used to be known as High Street House and its one room was home to George, his four brothers and sisters, his mother Mabel and his father Robert. Here in 1781 George was born and here he lived for the first few years of his life. The room is simply furnished in the style of its period, which Helen graciously explained to me, adding details of George's early life and then personal stuff about his later life. Great men and women frequently have inconspicuous beginnings and this place is one such. The pioneer of the railways, who later in life became very wealthy, investing in coal mines, railways and quarries, was inspired by the sight of those wagons that carried coal on the wooden track outside the place he knew as his first home.

I enjoyed Helen's narrative and went for the promised cup of tea in the garden behind the birthplace, before rejoining the course of the Hadrian's Wall Path across the Heddon golf course and up the hill into Heddon-on-the-Wall. The village itself appears to be some kind of posh outpost of Newcastle, even boasting a Shopping Centre, according to a signpost as you enter. Do not be deceived, for this turns out to be nothing more than a Spar shop behind the petrol station.

But, and it is a big but, here in Heddon is the first genuine stretch of the Wall to be seen. And it is magnificent. Situated to the east of the village on a quiet green, it is almost 100 yards long and in truth it's a bit of a shock when you finally get to it. All I'd read about its construction was there laid out in front of me. True, it's no longer at its full height but there was the ten foot breadth, there were the facing stones, there was the infilling with other stones and, yes, there was the Vallum behind it. I guess there must have been a milecastle here or hereabouts, as William Hutton also suggests, though he found the Wall here in 1801 to be "in a confused heap", unlike now. What I also liked about this stretch of the monument is that there was no obstacle to viewing it, no one trying to squeeze some cash out of you, no picture postcards or T-shirts or other tatty memorabilia. It was just Wall – plain, unadorned, and fascinating. I could almost see those squaddies from VI Victrix legion labouring away to construct their section of this monument to their Emperor Hadrian.

The track of the Wall for some distance out of Newcastle has been buried underneath the main A69 arterial road which connects the city to its west coast counterpart of Carlisle. When that road sweeps off to the north, it is replaced as a burial ground for the Wall by a minor road known as the Military Road, and the final stage of that day's walking was out of Heddon-on-the-Wall and along this Military Road, built by General Wade in the aftermath of the '45 rebellion so that armies could more quickly cross from east to west in the event of some subsequent invasion by the Jocks. I suppose it's not too surprising that one army preparing a defence should use the materials used by a previous army for the same purposes, but it's a bit of a shame for us as worshippers of historical monuments that Wade ordered his men to use the stones from Hadrian's Wall as the foundations for his Military Road. Consequently, for long stretches there's little evidence of the Wall itself. Fortunately, the Vallum and the ditch are both extensively evident, together with some other remains that help to give the overall picture.

One of these remains is at Rudchester, which is on the site of what used to be Vindobala fort. Excavations have shown that the fort was burned to the ground towards the end of the 2nd century, rebuilt shortly afterwards, abandoned a hundred years later, then strengthened and re-occupied until the withdrawal of the Roman legions in A.D. 411. The garrison in the 4th century comprised Frisians from Holland, who were notorious for wearing orange shirts all the time and speaking perfect English. They also planted tulips locally. Was it some of these Dutchmen who decided to bury some of the cohort's money beneath the floor of the nearest milecastle? We don't know of course, but in 1766 a couple of labourers dug up the buried cache of silver and gold coins, only to find them claimed by the estate's owner, who subsequently was forced to hand them over to the Duke of Northumberland. That's why the toffs always remain the toffs.

William Hutton in 1801 describes Rudchester as having "strong marks of former buildings, and still stronger of its ramparts". I walked around two sides of the oblong field that claims to be the site of the fort but could see nothing. I asked several sheep who were happily grazing there but they knew nothing either and so I concluded that the stonework had all been used to build Rudchester Hall, which abuts the field, and the Military Road.

And so to my resting place for the night, Ironsign Farm, on the site of a former inn built, inevitably, with stones from the Wall, just near the site of Milecastle 14. Originally two cottages, Ironsign was bought by Owen and Helen Little ten years ago and they have spent considerable time converting it. Originally it was to become a restaurant and that is still the intention but, with the coming of the National Trail past their door, they have started taking in travellers and that has become the dominant part of their trade. Owen was away at the time of my visit so I was looked after by his wife Helen.

"Can you recommend somewhere I can eat tonight?" I asked Helen, slightly anxious that this being Saturday night I might not be able to find much available.

"We usually send people to the Crown and Anchor at Horsley," she replied. "I'll give Brenda a ring if you like. She's ever so nice. I'm sure she can fit you in."

"Thanks, that's kind of you," I said and retired to my comfy room to get out of my walking gear and into something a little more Saturday nightish.

A bit later there was a knock at my door.

"Yes, that's alright now," Helen said. "I told her you'd be there about seven thirty. Is that OK? My son will take you and Brenda will bring you back."

I hadn't expected this. People down south on their first visit to the north often say that northerners are more friendly. Being a Midlander, where most people seem reasonably pleasant to each other, I find it hard to comment on this, but Helen's offer was the first of the many exceptional kindnesses I met on my walk along the Wall.

Young Owen duly drove me the couple of miles to the Crown and Anchor, where I was greeted by landlord Chris as if I was his long-lost mate from way back. Over my first pint of Bass, I got into conversation with Chris and another local couple about the growth in tourism brought about by the opening of the Hadrian's Wall Path. They were all happy that business was booming and were glad to welcome Wall walkers such as myself. I dined on an exquisite Northumbrian chicken which was smothered in a lovely thick sauce made from Lindisfarne Mead, had a further couple of pints of Bass to replace all the lost liquid of the day, and finished off with a brandy.

"Right, are you ready?" said Brenda, who had been supervising the busy kitchen, for the Crown and Anchor has a good clientèle apart from Wall walkers.

"I think so," I muttered, feeling replete. "That was delicious. Are you sure you don't mind? It might do me good to walk back after that meal."

"Don't be silly," she said. "I'll just bring the car round. It'll only take a few minutes to get you back."

And so, by nine thirty I was back in my room, watching an opening match of the European Football Championships between Spain and Russia. According to some experts, a troop of Spanish auxiliaries was stationed near here. What would they have made of their modern counterparts kicking an inflated pig's bladder around a grassy field, wearing baggy shorts and stripy shirts? They'd rather have seen the gladiators, I'm sure. I fell asleep dreaming of David Beckham as a gladiator. Don't ask. The beer had been very nice.

IV

HADRIAN THE IMMIGRANT

Hadrian, the mighty Roman Emperor, embodiment of all those Roman civic and military virtues, was actually a Spaniard. So, technically speaking, he was an immigrant. In less enlightened times, like our own perhaps, and from a less privileged background, he would have been classed as an asylum seeker and regarded as the lowest of the low.

It's not too surprising then to discover that the majority of the soldiers who were stationed on the Wall in its 300 or so years of existence were also not Roman; they were immigrants, like Hadrian himself. True, the Wall itself was built by the soldiers of the three legions stationed in Britain – II Augusta from Caerleon, XX Valeria Victrix from Chester and VI Victrix from York – and they were indubitably citizens of Rome, because that was the prequalification for being in the legions. But the manning of the Wall was given over to the auxiliary soldiers, who were in the first instance the young have-a-go heroes from conquered territories but later were often recruited from the native Brits themselves.

So, during the period of the Roman occupation, we had squaddies from Algeria, Belgium, Croatia, France, Germany, Holland, Hungary, Macedonia, Romania, Spain, Switzerland, Syria, Tunisia, Turkey and Yugoslavia stationed on the Wall. And don't tell me that multicultural mix didn't plant its seed in the native gene pool. Has there ever been a time when soldiers didn't spread their favours around? So let's have a look at some of these countries that the auxiliary squaddies came from and see what they might have brought with them to add to our cultural (and genetic) mix.

Given that Hadrian himself was from Italica near Seville, I have to start with the Spanish, don't I? There are records of cavalry troops from Asturia in north-west Spain at Benwell in Newcastle and at Chesters and Great Chesters forts in the early part of the 3rd century. Did they ride Spanish donkeys and wear pink sombreros? Did they have weekend rave-ups when they'd pour large amounts of Sangria down their throats and join in rapturous out-of-tune renditions of *Viva Espana*? Did they introduce the native Brits to *tapas* bars, QC sherry and tiny models of gaudily-dressed matadors?

It's worth pointing out that it took the Romans the best part of 200 years to conquer and subdue the Spanish tribes. The southern sea coast of Spain had long been fertile ground for seafaring settlers, or, depending on your point of view, raping and pillaging pirates, looking for new land and new trading possibilities. The Phoenicians were the first that we know about who created a town there, followed by the Greeks some time later, then crucially by the Carthaginians from northern Africa, who were after the rich seams of silver in the ground thereabouts. And, of course, with the Carthaginians we get Hannibal and his elephants; and no sooner have you got the Carthaginians than the Roman army has to have a good old ding-dong with them. Well, it wasn't quite like that time-wise but it's good enough for us to get the general picture. By about 200 B.C. the Carthaginians and their elephants had been driven out and Spain was technically a Roman province. This wasn't quite how the Spaniards saw it, of course, and they continued to rebel periodically just to keep the Roman army on its toes, until they finally gave in and decided to spend their time clacking their castanets, strumming their guitars and inventing Costa Lotta holidays.

I think you'll get some idea of why the Asturian cavalry were in Britain when I tell you that, once Spain was subdued, the only legion left there to keep it under check was VII Gemina which was based in León, the main city of this north-western territory. This served the dual purpose of helping to put down the revolting locals from time to time and of guarding the local gold mines, which were the most extensive in western Europe. And the best way to stop the locals from rebelling is to ship their boys off to another part of the Empire, kit them out with some flash uniforms and lure them with the promise of Roman citizenship 25 years down the line, if they're lucky enough to survive. The main effect of this heavy Roman presence in the area was that the locals forgot their own Celtic language and started speaking a sort of pidgin Latin which eventually turned into modern Spanish.

One of the Wall forts, Chesters, is known as Cilurnum, which curiously enough is a Celtic-Northumbrian term for a ladle. Why doesn't it have a Roman name like the other forts? Because the Asturians who manned it from the 3rd century onwards were descendants of a Celtic tribe known as the Luggones, literally the children of Lug, who were also known as the Cilúrnigos. Chesters fort, then, was almost certainly named Cilurnum by its Spanish auxiliary troops.

A further irony is that the Asturian region received a reverse flow of peoples from Britain some centuries later, when Britons fleeing the Saxon invasion fled south to find new land. There was even a bishopric in the area known as Bretonia. Nowadays half of the population of Essex seems to have upped sticks and bought villas in southern Spain, while there's a reverse flow of Spaniards moving to Britain to open tapas bars.

How curious the ebb and flow of history.

The greatest numbers of auxiliaries came, I suppose inevitably, from our nearest neighbour, France or Gallia, as Julius Caesar insisted on calling it. Gallia in the good old days included Belgium, bits of western Germany and chunks of northern Italy. As I've suggested earlier, the Gauls in many ways can be blamed for starting the Romans on their imperial pursuit, because it was the

Gauloise-smokers who first attacked Italy, turning Rome itself upside down in 390 B.C. and causing a right old panic. Even after they'd been thoroughly put in their place about a hundred years later by the burgeoning Roman army, they tried to sneak back on Hannibal's coat-tails (or rather his elephants' tails) after the Carthaginian had crossed the Alps. Sadly for them, Hannibal got thrashed and the Gallic threat was never quite the same thereafter. Having slunk back across the Alps, the defeated Gauls subsequently gave their undivided attention to shoulder-shrugging and existentialism. True, Julius Caesar seemed to spend a lot of his life dividing Gaul into three parts, as he was never tired of telling folk, and even more time writing his blasted book on the subject, in order to create tedious reading matter for wannabe Latin learners, like me aged eleven with the Reverend Rust.

France has sometimes been known as the breadbasket of Europe and there's no doubt that the Romans depended heavily on grain harvested and exported from Gaul to feed their troops all over the Empire. They also took a fancy to French cheeses, and it is likely that a lot of Roman armour was mass-manufactured at a centre in France. Masses of Samian pottery were made in France and exported all over the empire. In fact, wherever you find an archaeologist digging up bits of Roman history, you're almost certainly guaranteed a bit of that distinctive reddy-brown Samian pottery.

The biggest contingent of Gauls on the Wall was at Stanwix fort in present-day Carlisle. For most of the 300 years of Roman occupation there was a thousand-strong cavalry garrison stationed there. These were all auxiliaries, of course, not full legionaries, so you'll get some sense of how the Romans kept the young warriors away from their homelands if you think that each auxiliary retired after 25 years and had to be replaced. So that's a minimum of 12,000 Frenchmen required over the time of the Roman presence in Britain. Add to that the replacements that would have been necessary because of ill health retirement (probably quite common), battle scars retirement (also probably quite common, given that the Jocks were always causing a bit of hassle somewhere beyond the Wall), and accident retirement (falling off your horse, getting your arm ripped off in sword-drill, fooling about with your mates on top of the Wall), and you'll see that a substantial body of young Frenchmen was required regularly to do their military duty at Stanwix.

Segedunum, the Wallsend fort, was manned by Belgian troops in the 2nd century and by French ones in the third and fourth centuries. It seems pretty certain that both Housesteads and Vindolanda forts were manned at some stage by Tungrian soldiers from the area of Belgium now known as Louvain. The same area provided troops to Burgh-by-Sands fort in the 2nd century. So you see that there was a pretty strong French presence in Britain long before William came and conquered, and that presence would have found its way into the genetic pool, at least in the far north of England.

Some fifteen centuries after the Roman legions departed, there were still sufficient Gauls left in the north to staff every school in England with teachers of French.

The Germans were here too, of course, with their wonderful sense of humour and their penchant for curious moustaches. At various times there were soldiers from different Germanic tribes based at Wallsend, at Newcastle, at Great Chesters and at Burgh-by-Sands. Like everybody else in the history of Europe, the Romans had loads of trouble with the Germans. They were constantly crossing the River Rhine and threatening to pillage stuff that the Romans had themselves pillaged from the Gauls, until good old Julius Caesar took the offensive against them. The Emperor Augustus continued the process of trying to boss the Germans on a permanent basis but never really succeeded and, by the time of Hadrian, there was a sort of uneasy truce between the Roman Empire and the Germanic tribes, defined by the Rhine and the Danube and reinforced by the wooden palisade built on Hadrian's instructions – the predecessor of the Berlin Wall. So much trouble did the Germans cause Rome over a period of 200 years that there were no less than four legions permanently stationed there. Lower Germany was garrisoned by I Minervia and XXX Ulpia Victrix legions, while Upper Germania was garrisoned by VIII Augusta and XXII Primigenia legions. Both provinces were also supplemented by many auxiliaries.

The Roman historian Tacitus, you may be surprised to discover, was unwittingly responsible for Adolf Hitler. Tacitus's book *Germania* gives a description of the German people as he knew them (or, more likely, as he had read about them) in ways which modern readers will find uncomfortably close to those espoused by Hitler in his *Mein Kampf*. Here's Tacitus:

> *"I accept the view that the peoples of Germany have never contaminated themselves by intermarriage with foreigners but remain of pure blood, distinct and unlike any other nation."*

It is no accident that Hitler's notions of racial purity sound remarkably similar to Tacitus's view, for Hitler studied the Roman historian and used him to propound his own theories in *Mein Kampf*. He got a bit mixed up, however, for Tacitus's Germans had "fierce-looking blue eyes, reddish hair, and big frames", while Little Adolf went for the blond haired look himself. He also ignored the Roman writer's references to the German army's habit of chanting on the battlefield, unless you count "Gott in Himmel!" as a chant.

Apart from their policy of exporting the young German tough guys as auxiliary soldiers to the farthest points of the Empire to stop them fomenting trouble at home, the Romans also discovered a raw material in Germany which they found of massive value – amber. In Rome the price of amber was enormously high and only the super-rich could afford it. A small piece of amber, it is said, cost more than a good slave. Amber was believed to have exceptional medicinal qualities, whether worn around the neck to ward off tonsilitis or as beads to protect Roman women from thyroid disease. It was used to treat the symptoms of fever and as a medicine to eliminate that fever, and generally it was believed to protect people of all ages from "attacks of wild distraction", or what we might term barminess. Roman women held a piece of amber on their laps and stroked it in the belief that this would preserve their youthful looks. Emperor Nero's wife, Poppaea, was a big amber-stroker and a fashion setter, to the extent that many Roman women dyed their hair to match the colour of amber. Ain't fashion funny, eh?

One of the legions that served in Germany both before Hadrian's time and quite probably during it was the VIIII Hispana, or the infamous Ninth Legion, which inspired that terrific book, Rosemary Sutcliffe's *Eagle of the Ninth*. The Ninth Legion was one of the legions that came to Britain in Emperor Claudius's A.D. 43 invasion and was in Britain up to at least A.D. 108. We know that VIIII Hispana suffered heavy losses as a result of Boadicea's revolt but reinforcements were soon sent for and it was stationed at Lincoln until transferred to York in A.D. 71 to guard the northern frontier. The legion was involved in Agricola's campaigns into Scotland, it fought in the Battle of Mons Graupius in A.D. 82 and we know that it built a new fort at York in A.D. 108 And that's where the records get thin and the intrigue begins, because VIIII Hispana was replaced in York shortly afterwards and no one really knows what happened to it next. Some speculate that it was destroyed by the Jocks somewhere round about A.D. 118 and that this was the reason why Hadrian decided to build his Wall.

This indeed is the theory that fed Rosemary Sutcliffe's story about a young Roman soldier named Marcus, invalided out of his own battalion, setting out into the land of the Picts to retrieve the *aquila* (eagle) from the standard of VIIII Hispana which his father had commanded. Recent archaeological evidence, however, has destroyed that romantic notion, suggesting that the legion was active in Germany at a later period. That hasn't stopped the myth-makers, of course, and as I write there are three films – one of *Eagle of the Ninth* itself - currently being made about the Ninth Legion, which walked into the Scottish mist and was never seen again.

I think it's more likely they were eaten alive by the midges, but that wouldn't make a good movie, would it?

If you ever wondered where Richard O'Brien got his ideas for the *Rocky Horror Show* or Bram Stoker found the notion for *Dracula*, you need look no further than the Roman settlement at Birdoswald. For that fort was garrisoned in the 3rd century A.D. by auxiliaries from Dacia, or modern-day Transylvania in Romania, and I suspect both O'Brien and Stoker must have Transylvanian ancestry somewhere in their D.N.A. make-up, for both set their lurid tales in that scary kingdom.

The Dacians were not your typical barbarians. In fact, you could argue that their civilisation was at least as advanced as that of Rome when they first came into conflict in the 2nd century B.C. For 200 years the two empires recognised each other and sought some kind of co-existence, but it was never going to last. Emperor Trajan instituted two major campaigns to subdue the Dacians, finally succeeding in A.D. 106 when the Roman Empire's boundaries extended to reach the Carpathian mountains. Once the Romans got control, of course, the young bucks of Dacia were taken under their wing as auxiliaries and sent well away from home. Meanwhile, back in Dacia, the Romans began colonising, which in this case consisted of pocketing the gold and silver from the Carpathians - 165 tons of gold and 330 tons of silver found their way back to Rome after Trajan's conquest, as well as loads of iron. They then made the locals speak Latin. And that's why Romania is called what it is and why the language spoken by Ceaucescu and his nasty buddies was a romance lingo, directly evolved from Latin. So, *bună seara*, President Nicolae Ceaucescu and your lovely wife Elena. Hope you sleep well with the fishes.

The Dacian squaddies must have loved it at Birdoswald – lots of opportunities for swimming in the River Irthing, not far to walk to the pubs in Gilsland, nice views of the Pennines, and not the most dangerous of places as far as invading Jocks were concerned. So, plenty of time to dress up in their black togas, to stick some wild boar tusks either side of their mouths, and to scare all the locals when the moon was full. Or alternatively, to dress up in women's clothes and go and perform their version of the *Rocky Horror Show*. In Latin, of course.

The Pannonian auxiliaries, however, who came from the area that is now Hungary, were from a kettle of very different fish. We know that there was a squad of them stationed at one time at the no-longer visible Onnum fort between Rudchester and Chesters but they have even closer links with Hadrian. Lower Pannonia, whose main city was Aquincum, later to become Budapest, was the scene of Hadrian's first command as governor, appointed there about A.D. 107 by the Emperor Trajan. Pannonia remained one of Hadrian's favourite places and he often returned there later in his life, organising the building of many roads, temples, aqueducts, theatres and so on that helped to romanise the natives. On one occasion he witnessed a remarkable feat of endurance when a Batavian cavalry man named Soranus (I suspect there were other bits of him sore as well afterwards) swam across the Danube fully armed, as we read from his gravestone:

Here I am, who was famous in the whole of Pannonia.
Hadrian awarded the palm to me, when from Batavia's
Thousands of brave men, I succeeded in overcoming
The Danube deepness by swimming its waters in full armour.

This same Soranus had a pretty high opinion of himself, mind you, for he also claimed that he had split a falling arrow in two with his own arrow – a spot of Robin Hood type showing off there, I think – and that no Roman or anyone else could beat him in throwing the spear or shooting with his bow, never mind swimming. Good job he hadn't heard of Martin Strel then, a modern-day Pannonian, who currently holds the world record for non-stop swimming of 313 miles in 84 hrs and 10 min, in the River Danube, of course. This record was set in 2001 but the previous year Strel had swum the length of the Danube, all 1867 miles of it. Two years later he was at it again, this time swimming the 2360 mile length of the Mississippi in 68 days. Martin Strel's motto? 'Swimming for peace, friendship and clean waters.' Beats nuclear warfare.

Nowadays the British press is much exercised in scaring ordinary folk out of their wits with tales of asylum-seekers from Eastern Europe stealing our jobs, chatting up our women, and getting free brain transplants on our National Health Service. So it's ironic that troops from modern-day Hungary and Romania were stationed here all those years ago on Hadrian's Wall, and soldiers have never been famous for keeping their trousers on, have they? Around every Roman fort grew a civilian settlement and every civilian settlement would have had its fair share of prostitutes to service the squaddies. In addition it is almost certain that many of the auxiliaries took local women as their common-law wives and settled in the area where they had been stationed when they reached the end of their service in the army.

And it wasn't just Hungary and Romania that provided Eastern European troops; there were Thracians from modern-day Bulgaria and Turkey at Birdoswald, plus spotty Dalmatians from Croatia at Chesters and Carvoran. Then there were Tungrians on bicycles from Belgium at Vindolanda, at Birdoswald and at Burgh-by-Sands, Frisians with their cows from Holland at Housesteads and Rudchester, and yodelling Raetians from Switzerland at Great Chesters. And, even more interestingly, there were black Mauretanians from north Africa at Burgh-by-Sands and Hamian archers from Syria at Carvoran. The Wall was a melting-pot for soldiers from every part of the known world, and a right bunch they were too. What right did they think they had to protect us from the Jocks? Who gave them permission to get wounded or to die in our country? Who said they could live their fancy-Dan lives marching up and down the Wall, standing out in the freezing winds for hours on end on sentry duty with the wind whipping up their skirts, or getting shouted at by their Roman commanding officers for daring to question instructions? They should have bloody well thought themselves lucky not to be sent packing right away back where they came from. Personally, I blame that European Union (a.k.a. the Roman Empire).

But then again, I don't suppose we should be too surprised, when they let a Spaniard be the Roman Emperor.

How much did that multi-racial mix of soldiers stationed on Hadrian's Wall know about the Jocks they were there to keep out? Come to think of it, how much did Hadrian know of them? If he had read his Julius Caesar, he would have learned of the Britons' tendency to dye their bodies with woad, of their partiality for geese and for enjoying collective marriages. If he'd also read his Tacitus, he would have discovered that the Caledonians, as the Scotty tribes were known in those days, had red hair and large limbs and probably originated in Germany. But who were they really?

To be honest, we don't know a lot more than that. The Caledonians, or the Picts as they later became known, almost certainly were originally Celtic tribes who migrated from central Europe at some point of pre-history. They were farming folk, growing crops and keeping livestock. They were also nifty weavers, who created Harris Tweed and tartan scarves, leatherworkers, basketmakers, and inventors of shortbread biscuits. They had also developed skills in iron-making, not only for tins for the shortbread biscuits but three and a half foot longswords which put the frighteners on the renowned Ninth Legion.

Part of the enduring modern myth of Scotland is that its original inhabitants, these same Caledonians or Picts, were a democratic, freedom-loving people. Some of this owes its origin very much to Tacitus, who quotes the Caledonian leader Calgacus addressing his troops before the Battle of Mons Graupius as "the most distant dwellers upon earth, the last of the free" (you do wonder how Tacitus knew all this, when presumably Calgacus was speaking some kind of proto-Glaswegian). Other historians recorded that the Picts were a matrilineal society, i.e. that inheritance followed the mother of the family rather than the father, suggesting a more democratic ordering of things, which was complete nonsense. Just as in the Roman Empire, there was a rigid class system among the Jocks. The boss Jocks kept slaves from their own population and owned their own chariots.

So, the Jocks, whom Hadrian built his Wall to keep out, were not much different from the Hungarian, German, French, Romanian, Mauretanian, Syrian, Belgian, Dutch and Swiss soldiers who were actually on the Wall. True, the Roman auxiliaries had better armour and they had forts and the Roman army support network developed over some hundred or more years. True, the Roman weaponry was probably superior overall and their military capacity so much greater because of their history of conquest. True, as far as we know, the only ones to wear blue tattoos on their bodies were the Picts and remember:

> *Woad's the stuff to show men.*
> *Woad to scare your foemen.*
> *Boil it to a brilliant hue*
> *And rub it on your back and your abdomen.*
> *Ancient Briton ne'er did hit on*
> *Anything as good as woad to fit on*
> *Neck or knees or where you sit on.*
> *Tailors you be blowed !!*

But underneath all those tattoos and all that shiny armour, their societies were not that much different. What the Roman conquest created, and what Hadrian's Wall reinforced, was the notion of guerilla warfare, to be copied in our own times by the Vietcong and the Iraqis. Why take on the enemy in a pitched battle when they have greater physical resources than you? There's more ways than one to skin a cat, as the following story makes clear.

Before the Wall was built, the Roman and Scottish armies used to fight by gathering their armies on top of the hills and at day break running down the hillside into the gorges below to fight.

One morning at dawn there was a fog as thick as pea soup and the two generals decided to refrain from fighting that day. Whilst the two armies were resting a voice, with a Scottish accent, came from within the dense fog:

"Any one Jock can beat any ten Romans."

With this, the Roman general sent down ten of his soldiers. There was a hell of a fight and no-one returned. An hour later the same voice was heard:

"Any one Jock can beat any fifty Romans."

With this the Roman general sent down fifty of his soldiers. The same thing, a terrible fight ensured and again no-one returned. An hour later the same voice was heard again:

"Any one Jock can beat any hundred Romans."

The same thing again. Down went one hundred of the best. No-one returned. An hour later came the Scots voice again:.

"Any one Jock can beat any thousand Romans".

By this time, the Roman general had had enough and was about to send down his élite soldiers, when he saw a lone Roman soldier crawling up the hill. He was battered to a pulp.

As he reached his general he said:

"Don't send any more troops down, it's a trap. There's two of the buggers."

V

Chugging to Chesters

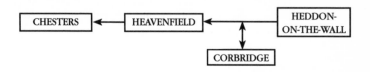

The next morning, I set off from Ironsign following a very filling breakfast. My walk was pleasant if largely uneventful and unremarkable, because of General George Wade. "Virginia" Wade was a career soldier who was sent to the Scottish Highlands in response to the 1715 Jacobite rebellion, to investigate the country and its people. Subsequently he oversaw the creation of the system of metalled roads to permit rapid movement of troops in order to quell the rebellious Jocks (yes, they were still causing trouble). These roads are his chief claim to fame and are commemorated in the lines:

> *"Had you seen these roads before they were made,*
> *You would lift up your hands and bless General Wade."*

Between 1724 and 1767 Wade and his successor, Major Caulfield, built 1200 miles of road and 700 bridges – a bit like the Roman army did, come to think of it - and in doing so they transformed the Highlands. Mind you, that didn't stop Bonnie Prince Charlie, who used those same roads to march rapidly into England and down to Derby. Wade was completely baffled by this, since his troops were in Newcastle and couldn't cross quickly enough to stop Charlie. So, after the Bonnie Prince had been seen off, Wade's response was to order the construction of the Military Road to connect Newcastle and Carlisle. It was done by using the available stone as its foundation, which was, of course, Hadrian's Wall, and it was this Military Road, now called the B6318, that I marched alongside that morning.

It's not especially inspiring here, except for the obvious presence of the ditch to your right and occasionally of the Vallum to your left. At times indeed you're actually walking in the ditch, a typical example of this being the stretch up to a hamlet called Harlow Hill, with its little church which is really a barn. This imaginative piece of re-use made me think of other possible Uses for Dead Churches and I whiled away the next part of my journey devising the following list:

1.   Lap dancing club
2.   Public convenience
3.   Tearoom
4.   Tory Party HQ
5.   Launchpad for British spaceship
6.   Tardis
7.   Refuge for asylum seekers
8.   Nuclear storage dump
9.   Skateboard park
10. Home for redundant royals, come The Revolution

Ah well, you can dream, can't you?

William Hutton records that there was a milecastle at Harlow Hill in 1801, surrounded by its own rampart, but there's no sign of that now. Hutton tells how he stopped a night here, with unforeseen results:

> *"Soliciting a bed, I was ushered into a parlour, where sat three gentlemen. I did not conceive I had a right to intrude, so took my place at the greatest distance. A suspicious silence immediately surrounded their little table. As I never made a secret of myself, or the plan I was pursuing, I endeavoured to introduce a communication, for truth makes a wonderful impression upon the mind; when, after an hour or two's chat, one of them remarked, 'You are the most agreeable companion I have met with;*

> *but, I do assure you, when you first entered, I took*
> *you for a spy employed by the Government."*

I looked around the few houses but there was no sign of life at that time on this Sunday morning. I looked back down the road towards Heddon and forwards in the direction I was heading and, as I did so, I was passed by a clutch of black-jacketed motorcyclists – Sunday BAMBIs (Born Again Middle-aged Bikers) using the Military Road as their race track. They did not stop, so there was no one who might have mistaken me for a Government spy. I breathed a great sigh and continued on my journey.

In a while, still following the Military Road, you come downhill towards the Whittle Dene reservoirs which provide water to Newcastle and Gateshead. A couple of fishermen were staring moodily into the waters there, hoping for some roach or gudgeon to fasten itself on to their hooks but unaware, I guess, of the interesting scientific study that is being carried out here. The Whittle Dene Project is exploring the impact on water supplies of the sorts of pesticides and fertilisers commonly used by farmers in their search for higher yields. Now you'd think they knew about that from laboratory experimentation, wouldn't you? But the point of this work is that it will be measuring the pace at which such pesticides and other pollutants enter the water and their relative strength on entry. 200 miles away in a research lab. in Nottinghamshire, scientists in white coats (Drs. Bunsen Honeydew and Beaker) will be studying the results by triggering the automatic instruments inserted in the Whittle Dene reservoirs and in the nearby streams and burns. Fascinating, eh?

These reservoirs are also a favourite haunt of twitchers like Bill Oddie, particularly in winter when birds in flight are attracted by the shiny water. On one Sunday in January this year, for instance, the following were all seen at Whittle Dene: American wigeon, whooper swan, goosander, smew, pink-footed goose, green sandpiper, wigeon, goldeneye, tufted duck, mallard, coot, pochard, grey heron, cormorant, greylag goose, grey wagtail, rook, pheasant.

I winged it on to the Robin Hood Inn, a delightful old pub built, so I'm told, with stones from the Wall. The Robin Hood is one of the stops for those who seek to prove that they have walked this long-distance path by stamping their Hadrian's Wall Path Passport at six points along the Wall. I stopped for a coffee instead and sought the reason for this Northumbrian pub bearing the name of the legendary Sherwood Forester. The barman didn't know but thought there was some old story that Robin Hood had once operated in this territory.

In recent years there has been a campaign to place him and his Merrie Men in Yorkshire and I suppose that Yorkshire could do with some Merrie Men but it sounds to me like a bit of a swiz really. Everyone knows that Robin Hood comes from Nottinghamshire, don't they? Now here was Northumberland laying claim to being the bold robber's homeland. In truth, of course, there probably never was a real Robin Hood, but there almost certainly were feudal English lords driven out of their homes by the Norman Conquest and intent on reclaiming their lands. So it's just as likely that there was such a character in the ancient kingdom of Northumbria. And in Yorkshire. And in Nottinghamshire. And in Wolverhampton too, probably.

A little further on, just past Carr Hill, I crossed into a field where a spectacular section of the Vallum can be seen. It's only when you see the sheer size of the Vallum that you begin to wonder what its real purpose was. After all, it was built to the south of the Wall in land which the Roman army controlled, unlike the dangerous lands to the north where the Jocks were plotting mischief. Did the Romans expect attacks from the rear from some disaffected Brits? Maybe some latter-day Boadicea intent on gaining revenge? Were the conquered Brits trying to smuggle out the secret recipe for pork scratchings? Or was this just to mark out the full extent of the military territory perhaps? Again, as with so much of the Wall, we really don't know.

At the huge gateway that marks the road up to Halton Castle,

I encountered a gaggle of women who had just finished the circular walk to Corbridge, having had to miss this out when they completed their four-day walk along the Wall path the previous Easter.

"Was it worth it then? I asked.

"No," one of them replied. "I turned down the chance of a Roman orgy in Wallsend to come here. Now I wish I hadn't."

You meet all sorts, don't you?

Halton Castle is a pele tower attached to a farmhouse, both built inevitably with stones from Hadrian's Wall. Pele towers, named after their Brazilian inventor of course, were built in this part of the north in the Middle Ages to enable their owners to spy out trouble that might be coming from the north, for this was the time of the notorious Reivers, whom I promise I will introduce to you more fully at a later stage in this narrative. For now all you need to know is that these Reivers were basically rustlers and that the occupier of Halton Castle in 1276 was Sir John Halton, who was the Sheriff of Northumberland. This didn't stop him doing a spot of rustling himself, mind you, though he wasn't very good at it. One day he stole some cattle from a neighbour but was caught doing it and brought before his own court for punishment. His position saved him from the gallows but he had to fork out a fair amount of groats in recompense to his angry neighbour.

We all know how unusual it is for law enforcement officers to commit criminal acts, don't we? Ho, ho.

The Errington Arms, where a short time later I paused to eat my packed lunch and sup a couple of pints of Jennings's Cumberland Ale, was the ancestral home of the Errington family, who can trace their origins to Orm of Errington in 1181, who was probably of Saxon ancestry. The Erringtons were fighting men, one of them being with Henry V at Agincourt, others being heavily involved in the Civil War, and another scion of the family joining Bonnie Prince Charlie in the '45 Jacobite Rebellion and seizing Holy Island Castle.

The Errington Arms stands at Portgate, which is the point where the Military Road is crossed by Dere Street, the great supply road that carried goods and men from York north into Scotland and back again. From here it's about three miles down Dere Street to Corbridge, which was where the main supply fort on the eastern side of the Wall was situated. Corbridge, or Corstopitum as it was known, is remarkably well preserved.

On the way to Corbridge you pass what is now a rather nondescript Stagshaw Bank on your right hand side. This for centuries was the scene of two great annual fairs held on the day before Whit Sunday and on July 4th. These were reputed to be the largest single-day fairs in the whole of England, but died out in the 19th century. Stagshaw Fair must have been a wonder to behold, with its stalls selling hats, boots and shoes, jewellery and hardware, saddlery and farming goods, cooperage goods such as tubs and barrel churns, webs of cloth and the famous Hexham Tan gloves, which gave you an instant suntan a lot cheaper than an hour at the Corbridge Tantastic. There was also the usual assembly of shysters seeking to get punters' money in a variety of ways, such as Billy Purvis, who, with "painted face and gaudy clothes" invited you into his little booth where he performed "wonderful sleight-of-hand tricks, without the aid of apparatus". There were also collections of wild beasts, usually monkeys of some sort or other, for our forefathers were not as squeamish as we are about displaying wild animals for amusement.

As you pass this now-silent place, it is hard to imagine how central to people's lives were these annual fairs across Britain. The hustle and bustle have gone the way of the garrisons on Hadrian's Wall. All that are left are ghosts.

Modern Corbridge is rather twee, with its tea shoppes and its upmarket ambience but it is the site of the Roman fort that is its main reason for existence. Corstopitum was built at the time of Agricola's northwards advance and is the eastern end of the Stanegate, the military route built at the same time to connect with Stanwix in the west. It would appear that the fort was abandoned at the time of the building of Hadrian's Wall but it later became a major supply depot, housing a large civil as well as military population. The museum that you explore on entering the site has some fine excavated findings, including the usual Samian pottery, a few coins, a neat collection of tools and instruments, and some tombstones. There's also some rather exquisite jewellery and a reproduction of the most famous finding from the site – the Corbridge Lion, which is a beautifully-wrought carving of a lion crouching over its stag prey and is thought to have come from the mausoleum because of the association in Roman times of the lion and its prey with death.

The site of the fort itself, however, is something else and gives you a far better sense of fort buildings than the shadowy outlines at Segedunum do, mainly because the excavations discovered many of the foundations and lower stages of the buildings virtually intact. Almost as soon as you come out of the museum you're on the Stanegate itself, now slightly wobbly because of the subsidence of centuries. The paving stones aren't as regular or as well spaced and preserved as a street in Pompeii, for instance, but this is unmistakably a street and it is unmistakably Roman-straight. From here it would have headed west towards Carlisle. If you stare into the distance, you can imagine dust raised by the marching troops and the supply wagons as they leave Corbridge. At right angles to the Stanegate would have run Dere Street heading for the Wall and all points north, its opposite end crossing the River Tyne to the south - you can still see some of the bridge abutments at low tide.

The foundations of two massive granaries dominate the remains at Corbridge, showing that it must have been of major importance in the storage of grain for troops at the further advanced forts, as well, perhaps, as feeding the local civilian population. Here you can see Roman architecture at its best, with the raised granary floors clearly in evidence to allow air to circulate underneath the grain to keep it dry. It is reckoned that it would have taken something like 10,000 soldiers to man the Wall, so, when you envisage these huge granaries and realise that they would probably have had to store grain for maybe one third of those squaddies, you can see why they needed to be so big.

Another interesting feature of Corstopitum is the outline of a *mansio*, or inn, alongside the Stanegate. The imperial postage system, the *cursus publicus*, which was the forerunner of the Pony Express, had *mansiones* throughout the Empire. These acted as posting-houses and as places of rest for those travelling with correspondence, where they could exchange their weary horses, and for other Roman citizens travelling with official goods or on official business. They were the Travelodges of their day, really, where no doubt weary travellers could get a bite to eat, a glass or two of the local poison, and a video of *Gladiator* to send them to sleep. Quite why there is a *mansio* in Corstopitum has never been explained, but it may simply have been an official residence for important visitors travelling along the Stanegate or Dere Street.

There are other worthwhile sights in Corstopitum, including an underground treasure house, where the army's pay would have been stored, and the remains of a fountain, into which the squaddies would chuck three coins and make a wish, which would have been fed by some elaborate waterworks system from a nearby spring. There's also evidence that, certainly in its later manifestation, Corstopitum had a substantial civilian population. In the foundations of several of the buildings running either side of the Stanegate were found tools and remnants that suggest these housed leather-workers, smiths and potters. In one of these, the original excavations found large amounts of pottery as if it had fallen off the shelves on which it had been stored, presumably because of some major Jock invasion.

Corstopitum is a rather fine site, the first excavated fort on the journey west from Wallsend, and gives a superb feel for the nature of such forts. It's easy to get misty-eyed about such things when you visit somewhere like this but, on the day I was there, standing high above the River Tyne in the sunshine, I could easily envisage a legion marching over the bridge towards the fort, weary after their several days' travel from York – the sound of marching feet, the flash of armour, the legion's flag preceding the footsore soldiers, the barked commands of the centurions.

Eat your heart out, Rosemary Sutcliffe!

Back on the main route the next significant site is that of the Battle of Heavenfield. With a name like that it's not too surprising that this insignificant field should lay claim to being responsible for bringing Christianity to Britain.

How come? Pin back your ears and I'll tell you.

Picture this. It's the early 7th century, the Romans have been gone over 300 years and the Angles, Saxons and Jutes have spread across the land, pushing the Celts and Britons back into Wales and Scotland. The Celt Cadwallon of Gwynedd decides to take on these foreigners and advances northwards into Northumbria, which in those days stretched from Edinburgh down to the River Humber. Top dog among the Northumbrians is a certain Oswald, who had been brought up by the Christian monks on Iona. In A.D. 633 "Ossie" has returned to Bamburgh Castle, the traditional home of the Northumbrian kings, and now marches south to rally his troops in the north Tyne valleys. Cadwallon has marched north from his headquarters in York and the two armies have decided to have a bit of a barney here at what is now known as Heavenfield.

If you stand by the very helpful sign where this information is displayed, you can see St. Oswald's church at the top of the hill to the north. On this site, the night before the battle, "Ossie" planted a wooden cross and made his men take their caps off and pray for victory. Whether it was because he had God on his side, or whether Cadwallon's troops were knackered from walking all the way from York, or whether they got trapped in front of Hadrian's Wall which was then probably still standing to its full height, or whether it was just a bad day at the office for Cadwallon the Celt, we don't know. But win "Ossie" did and one of his first acts was to get the Iona monks, with St Aidan as their leader, to start a monastery on Lindisfarne.

And the rest, as they say, is history, as Christianity spread throughout the country, like foot-and-mouth disease. At least, that's the version that the Venereal Bede tells us but the reality is less straightforward, since Cadwallon himself, it is thought, was a Christian. What is definitely true is that "Ossie" became St. Oswald, while Cadwallon became dead meat.

A bit further on you come to another surprising section of the Wall. This section, some thirteen yards long, owes its survival to William Hutton who, on arriving here on his epic journey in 1801, found some 95 yards of the Wall had already been demolished by a certain Henry Tulip Esq. (descendant of a Dutch auxiliary) in order to build himself a new farmhouse, probably the nearby Planetrees Farm. Hutton was mighty upset at this destruction and sent a message to the aforesaid Henry Tulip via the servant who was doing the demolition work:

> *"Give my compliments to Mr Tulip, and request him to desist, or he would wound the whole body of Antiquities. As he was putting an end to the most noble monument of Antiquity in the whole Island, they would feel every stroke. If the wall was of no estimation, he must have a mean opinion of me, who would travel six hundred miles to see it; and if it was, he could never merit my thanks for destroying it."*

According to Hutton, the servants ceased their demolition work there and then, which is why this section of the Wall stands proud and alone in its field, awaiting inspection from the likes of me and other latter-day Huttons.

It's only another mile or so till you come to a minor diversion whose purpose at first you cannot ascertain. This takes you around the perimeter of the territory of Brunton House, where I guess the Bruntons do not wish to be disturbed by oiks in cagoules and walking boots, and back into Chollerford. The reason for the diversion is to take you past Brunton Turret. Or at least the remains of the Brunton Turret. And here is a real piece of excitement for all Wall-anoraks everywhere, because here there is evidence of the ten-foot Wall and of the eight-foot Wall. Wowee! This is what we've been waiting for!

What you can see is how the foundation stones of the Wall are ten feet across and how the stones of the actual Wall, laid on top, are only eight feet across. And you do begin to question why the original plan was changed and when. What the stonework here suggests also is that the initial line of the Wall was laid out by one bunch of squaddies, while a later group finished it off. Let's not forget the turret itself, which is one of the best-preserved on the whole length of the Wall. While the remnants of the Wall here are up to six courses high, the turret rises to eleven courses in places and you get a pretty good sense of how small this part of the Wall system was and how this was really little more than a guarding post, filled, I would guess, by one or two squaddies at a time on duty, scratching themselves and wishing they were back home.

And so on over Chollerford Bridge and past the George Hotel, which claims to have accommodated, on separate occasions, the three great writers, Rudyard Kipling, J. B. Priestley and George Bernard Shaw. As a result of his visit to this spot near the line of Hadrian's Wall, Kipling wrote an atmospheric piece called On The Great Wall in his children's book, *Puck of Pook's Hill*. Here's a bit of it for your delectation:

"But the wall itself is not more wonderful than the town behind it. Long ago there were great ramparts and ditches on the South side, and no one was allowed to build there. Now the ramparts are partly pulled down and built over, from end to end of the Wall; making a thin town eighty miles long. Think of it! One roaring, rioting, cock-fighting, wolf-baiting, horse-racing town, from Ituna on the West to Segedunum on the cold eastern beach! On one side heather, woods and ruins where Picts hide, and on the other, a vast town – long like a snake, and wicked like a snake. Yes, a snake basking beside a warm wall!"

Oh, Mr. Kipling, you do write exceedingly strange things. A snake basking beside a warm wall? What's that all about? You should stick to making cakes.

The George was also the site of a meeting between James Radcliffe, 3rd Earl of Derwentwater, and fellow conspirators to plot their part in the Jacobite Rebellion of 1715 to put James Stuart on the English throne. The uprising failed, of course, and Radcliffe was beheaded on Tower Hill in London in February 1716. It is rather ironic that these enemies of King George II did their plotting in a remote inn which would later become known as The George.

The George Hotel was too full to accommodate me, either for a bed or for a meal, so I had found other accommodation at Green Carts Farm, but first I had to visit one of the great treasure houses on Hadrian's Wall – the Roman fort of Cilurnum, or Chesters as it is better known.

I really should have visited Chesters the following day which was a Monday. Let me explain my reason. The person responsible for uncovering Chesters fort in the first place was a gent called John Clayton who inherited the estate from his father Nathaniel. John

Clayton was a seriously busy bloke. He trained as a lawyer and entered his father's law firm, where he became head of chambers in 1832. He was also Town Clerk of Newcastle, in which position he was responsible for much of the redevelopment of Newcastle in the 1830s and 1840s. However, he had become fascinated with the Roman remains uncovered when his father started landscaping the Chesters estate, and set himself to excavate as much as possible within the grounds. He did this on Mondays, in the way that only Victorian gentlemen of a certain style could do. From 1843 till his death in 1890 Clayton uncovered virtually the whole of the Chesters site that you can see today.

Clayton became fascinated with Hadrian's Wall and was not satisfied with excavating only Chesters but, thanks to his growing wealth in Newcastle, he set himself to preserve as much of the remains of the Wall as he could find. In his lifetime he bought up land along the Wall between Brunton in the east and Cawfields in the west, thus taking ownership of not only Chesters but also Carrawburgh, Housesteads and Vindolanda. It is largely thanks to John Clayton that so much of Hadrian's Wall has been preserved for us to gawp at now. Without him there would have been no Chesters, no Housesteads, no Vindolanda, and no Hadrian's Wall Path for me to traipse along.

Chesters fort is one of the largest on the line of the Wall and is, according to the official guidebook, the best example of a cavalry fort visible anywhere in the Roman Empire. To get into Chesters, you have to pay your entrance money to a very nice lady who showed me where I could stow my rucksack, then pass through a picnic site till you reach the remains of the North Gate. Standard stuff this, if you know your Roman fort layout (and you should by now, after visiting Segedunum and Corbridge). The gateway has a guard-room on either side and there would have been a walkway on ramparts above it. However, the East Gate probably is the most interesting because here Clayton's meticulous excavations showed how the gate had been modified at different periods of the fort's existence. Nothing unusual in that, I suppose. No doubt the Romans had the same urge to change their habitations from time to time as we do and no doubt each fort would have had a style guru to advise them on what looked prettiest at the time.

You can happily spend a couple of hours at Chesters, as I did, for there is lots to wander around and try to make sense of. It really is a very large site, as the official guidebook points out, but its glory has to be the Bath House, situated on a quarried-out shelf of land just down from the bridge across the River North Tyne, the abutments of which are still visible. This is the bath house which was used as the model for the reconstruction at Segedunum where I had undertaken my imaginary cleansing a couple of days previously. You enter these substantial remains down a flight of steps which lead to the entrance hall which was the main changing room. There are still the niches in the wall where bathers would dump their togas before leaping into the *frigidarium* (cold bath) with shouts of "Bloody hell! This is Britain, isn't it? Do we really need this?" Then comes the *tepidarium* (warm room), followed by the caldarium (hot room), before you return to the changing room for a bit of a gossip about hard times on the Wall, swapping news about your haemorrhoids, and boasting about your latest sexual conquest down in the civilian settlement near the George Hotel.

The Chesters museum is a very strange beast altogether. Some people I met there were enthralled by it but I was personally less intrigued, mainly because it is so cramped and the notion of laying exhibits out in a way that is helpful to those with only a fleeting knowledge of all things Roman seems to have bypassed the museum's creators. I suspect this is pretty much as it was when John Clayton collected everything together in the first place, for it bears the hallmark of the sort of museums that used to put me off when I was a schoolboy. Now I know that it's quite easy to overdo the whizzbangery and the touchy-feely videos stuff, but it's a shame that English Heritage, who now look after Chesters, don't spend a bit of cash bringing all these wonderful findings into some kind of shape that tells more of a story.

For instance, there's a fine statue found in the baths of the Commandant's House. This, you are told, could either be Neptune or a "personification" of a River God of the Tyne which flows 150 yards from the baths. And you want to ask, so what? Tell me what the significance of all that is, even if you're only speculating. Then there are two building stones with startlingly clear images of wild boars on them, one of which bears the legend XXVV. This, you learn, means it was placed by the XX Valeria Victrix legion but again I want to ask, so what?

Now I know, because I've been reading about it, that the XX Valeria Victrix was one of the Roman army's crack troops. It served first in the Emperor Augustus's long campaign against the Spanish, then later was transferred to the Balkans. The Emperor Tiberius deployed the legion in his great war on the eastern front of the Empire, where it served with distinction, and it later served in Germany. It was one of the legions brought over to Britain in Claudius's campaign to conquer the island and, after the early success of that campaign, was initially based at Colchester. It is believed that XX Valeria Victrix may have been the legion involved in putting down Boadicea; at any rate, it definitely marched north some years later with Agricola and from its temporary base at Carlisle was part of Agricola's campaigns in Scotland. In A.D. 88 the legion was sent to what became its new permanent base at Chester, from where it was ordered some thirty or so years later to join in the construction of the central section of Hadrian's Wall. Its symbol was a jumping boar.

If I can find that much, don't you think the punters who pay their money to English Heritage deserve something similar?

Elsewhere in the museum there's lots of iron objects – keys, hooks, chains, nails and so on – just crying out for something more than being displayed altogether in a glass case. There's lots of pottery too – figurines of I know not what, finely decorated pots and earthenware items – in a case with whetstones and, for some unknown reason, a boar's jawbone. None of it is fully explained and it's such a shame, because bringing the Roman experience to life should be the purpose of such museums.

I had a cup of tea and a slice of delicious carrot cake at the Chesters tearoom and scribbled down my thoughts on the site. I admit I was frustrated and a bit angry. The potential of Chesters is huge but it needs someone to kick ass and make it happen.

I was only a short distance from my night's resting place at Green Carts Farm and was trudging up the road from Chesters in its direction when a car pulled up beside me.

"Are you Bob Bibby?" asked the middle-aged woman driving.

"I am," I said.

"Are you heading for Green Carts?"

"I am," I answered. "Why? Are you Sandra Maughan?"

"That's me," she replied. "Get in. I'll give you a lift. It's only just up the road."

I climbed into the battered old car, squeezing my rucksack on to my knee.

"I passed you going the other way," Sandra said. "I was taking Canadians to the pub. Will you be going there this evening? I can take you."

I've already mentioned the kindness of people I met on my trek and Sandra Maughan provided another remarkable example.

"I tried to get into The George for a meal," I explained. "But they said they were full."

"Well, you'll be better off at The Hadrian," Sandra said. "They do good meals there. You'll probably meet the Canadians. I've just taken them there."

I muttered my thanks.

"That's alright," she said, steering the car into the farmyard, where chickens scattered. "There's nowhere else round here. Get yourself changed and I'll run you down. I'll pick you all up later on, when you're ready."

And that's why later that Sunday evening I was sat in the garden of The Hadrian Hotel in a place called, appropriately enough, Wall, sipping a final glass of brandy as the sun set on what had been a glorious day's weather. I had dined on a delicious Hadrian's Cod, which was covered in cheese sauce and pink prawns, and drunk three pints of Jennings's Cumberland Ale. I felt full and happy.

Shortly afterwards Sandra arrived, with a slightly bigger car this time, to collect the three Canadians and myself for the homeward journey. Back in my comfy room I switched on the TV to watch the England-France match in the European Championships – a match which England should have won but contrived to lose. I thought how fitting it was that the climax of my day in this most northerly part of England should be spent watching the Gauls, who were one of the auxiliary groups that were stationed here, beating the Britons, who were living in the surrounding hills and valleys. Even more pertinent was the fact that both teams comprised a goodly number of black players, descendants perhaps of those African auxiliaries who also served on the Wall and, like their modern counterparts, learned the ways of the Roman conquerors and adapted their own lifestyles to fit in. Who knows? Some of those African soldiers may well have also turned out to be better warriors that their Roman counterparts. And, if the stories are true, they may certainly have been better lovers.

VI
HADRIAN THE HUNK

Compared with his predecessors, Hadrian was remarkably restrained as far as his sex life was concerned. Julius Caesar set the precedent with his numerous conquests both at home and abroad. He seduced the wives of many of his fellow-senators, including the wife of Cràssus, who would later be one of the conspirators responsible for his death. Probably not a good move then. In the provinces, Caesar had a reputation for having his wicked way with the queens of conquered nations, the most famous of whom, of course, was the beautiful Egyptian Cleopatra. The historian Suetonius tells us of a verse sung about Julius during his triumphs in Gaul:

> *We're bringing home the bald adulterer;*
> *Romans, keep your wives indoors.*
> *The gold you lent him here at home*
> *Has all been spent on Gallic whores.*

Tiberius was even wilder, retiring to the Isle of Capri to indulge himself in sexual extravaganzas with the collection of young girls and young boys gathered from all over the Empire whom he called his *spintriae*. In his palatial villa high in the hills, he had rooms decorated with indecent pictures and rude statues. He had young girls dress up as nymphs and then chased them into various caves around the island where he ravished them. He trained little boys to lick his penis while he was swimming. In short, he was a thoroughly vile human being.

Caligula was no better. He committed incest with his sisters, one of them when he was still under age, and had homosexual relationships with actors, foreign hostages, and other Roman nobles. He was notorious for inviting leading Roman citizens to dinner with their wives then picking out one of the women and taking her off for a quickie, before returning and discussing her merits with the rest of his guests. On one occasion he attended the wedding of a Roman noble and after the ceremony carted off the poor man's wife to his own bedroom, only to send her away a few days later when his appetite was sated.

But the worst of the lot was Nero, whose lasciviousness knew no bounds and who became known as the ultimate in sexual deviance. His public dinner parties were attended by dancing girls and prostitutes. When sailing down the Tiber, he had brothels erected along the shore where noblewomen, posing as prostitutes, would thrust their bare breasts at him to solicit his custom. Not content with having his way with young boys, prostitutes and other people's wives, he raped one of the Vestal Virgins. He had a young boy called Sporus castrated then went through a wedding ceremony with him/her, bridal veil and everything. Later he was himself married to another boy called Doryphorus and on the wedding night imitated the screams of a young girl being deflowered. To top all this, he slept with his own mother Agrippina. No wonder Rome burned down on his watch.

Many historians believe that Rome was a den of vice and indeed that is substantially the thesis advanced by Edward Gibbon in his seminal work *The Decline and Fall of the Roman Empire*. Gibbon argued that the Roman Empire would have lasted longer if its emperors had stuck to their hunt for pork scratchings rather than indulging their carnal lust. There is certainly no doubt that the emperors weren't alone in their debauchery, though it seems likely that sexual extravagance was most likely to be found among the wealthy, as is the way the world over.

Dancing girls, who were slaves brought from all corners of the Empire, performed at dinner parties and private do's, wearing skimpy costumes and dancing erotically. If you thought that lap-dancing clubs were a modern invention, just listen to the Roman poet Juvenal's description of such girls:

> *"Perhaps you will expect the itching dances of Gades,*
> *while a band croons, and the girls sink to the ground*
> *and quiver to applause...a stimulus for languid lov-*
> *ers, nettles to whip rich men to life."*

Prostitution was rife in Roman society and not regarded as anything abnormal. It was considered usual for young men to visit prostitutes when they were still single. All prostitutes were slaves and each had a particular beat. Some wandered the streets at night and were known as *noctilunae* (night moths); others, known as *bustuariae* (grave-watchers), hung around in cemeteries, pretending to be professional mourners at a funeral then offering some light relief to any of the assembled males who needed to relieve their distress on the nearest gravestone.

Brothels, called *lupinaria*, were sited close to the Circus Maximus in order to attract men on their way out after being excited by the sadistic pleasures of the gladiatorial contests. I've never noticed any brothels near Wembley Stadium or Lord's Cricket Ground (or, come to think of it, near Molineux Stadium) but I bet they exist. The brothel in Pompeii is one of the most visited features of that famous site. Modern-day tourists normally have to queue to get inside the tiny building with its dimly-lit rooms decorated with obscene pictures and rude graffiti, such as:

> *"Here Harpocras has had a good shag with Drauca for*
> *a denarius."*

Or:

> *"Myrtis, you do great blow jobs."*

It's not too surprising then to find that the phallus was a symbol of everything positive in the Roman Empire. Not just brothels, but shops and houses too displayed large pictures of an upright phallus with the logo *Hic habitat felicitas* (Here lies happiness). It was the ultimate symbol of power, luck, and fertility. The Romans believed that the male member was the source of life and the bigger the better.

History has not recorded the dimensions of Hadrian's genitalia but he was reasonably normal in his sexual life, for a Roman at any rate. He married Sabina, the niece of Emperor Trajan, in 100 A.D, when he was twenty-four and she fourteen. Nothing unusual in that, for this was an arranged marriage in the tradition of those days. Marriage contracts were determined by the two families, with an eye to securing their financial well-being and status. At the betrothal, Hadrian would have given Sabina an iron ring and placed it on the fourth finger of her left hand while the contract was drawn up, and a ceremony would have been conducted in front of invited guests, followed by a bit of a bean-feast with lots of wine and posh nosh.

On the day of the wedding itself, Sabina would have been dressed by her bridesmaids in a white tunic, fastened by a woollen belt, with an orange-red veil over her head and orange-red shoes and her hair would have been elaborately coiffed. Hadrian would have led the procession to her family home, where the two would have made solemn declarations confirming their acceptance of the marriage contract, their hands would have been joined together, and the priest would have said a quick how's your father. This would have been followed by the traditional booze-up, or marriage banquet, with all the guests regaling themselves with forgotten moments from previous wedding feasts and generally getting slaughtered, before Hadrian and Sabina, preceded by flute-players and torch-bearers would have been led to their new home. Here Hadrian would have lifted his new wife over the threshold, as it was considered bad luck if she tripped there, and taken her into the house, where he would have loosened her belt and she would have taken her tunic off before sitting naked on the phallus of the god of fertility, named Mutumus Tutumus. And then he would have given her a good seeing to.

Whether Sabina enjoyed it or not was irrelevant. Even in those days, faking it was considered a good thing, as the poet Ovid points out in his advice to young lovers:

> *"Coax and flatter and tease, with inarticulate mur-*
> *murs, even with sexual words, in the excitement of*
> *play, and if nature, alas, denies you the final sensa-*
> *tion cry out as if you had come, do your best to pre-*
> *tend … if you have to pretend, be sure the pretence is*
> *effective, do your best to convince, prove it by rolling*
> *your eyes, prove by your motions, your moans, your*
> *sighs, what a pleasure it gives you."*

That was it. Nothing out of the ordinary there. Hadrian merely doing what a man's gotta do, and Sabina responding appropriately. Except that, in normal circumstances, Sabina would at some point shortly afterwards have started producing little sprogs. Possible future emperors. But that never happened and we don't learn much about Sabina except almost in parenthesis. You'll remember, perhaps, that she came to Britain with Hadrian just before he set in motion his super new scheme to build a Wall across the north of the land, and that his letter-writer Suetonius was dismissed for some alleged hanky-panky with the Empress. You will be interested to know that Hadrian considered dismissing his wife too "for being moody and difficult", and would have done so if he'd been a private citizen. Elsewhere Sabina was more open about the reasons for her behaviour towards Hadrian and for her failure to bear children:

> *"She used to boast that she had taken steps to make*
> *sure she did not become pregnant by him – offspring*
> *of his would harm the human race."*

So what might these steps that Sabina took have been? Sexual restraint was unlikely, for Roman emperors, as we've seen, were notoriously incapable of keeping their genitals inside their pants. However, we do know that *coitus interruptus* was practiced, as a Roman writer called Soranus tells us:

> *"At the critical moment of coitus, when the man is about to discharge the seed, the woman should hold her breath and hurl herself away a little so that the seed may not be lodged too deeply within the cavity of the uterus. Then the woman should immediately get up and squat down, induce sneezing, and wipe the vagina (clean) all around and maybe drink something cold."*

Iced capuccino? Or maybe some nice cool Irn-Bru, specially imported from Jockland?

The same writer advises the use of various ointments smeared on the mouth of the uterus, such as old olive oil, honey, cedar resin, or the juice of a balsam tree. Other gums and resins were supposed to act as spermicides, while various vaginal suppositories like a lock of fine wool or white lead were also suggested as effective means of effecting birth control. A number of herbal concoctions were also supposed to have similar effects, although Soranus warns that there could be serious side-effects, like nausea, damage to the stomach, congestion of the head, and other problems.

One of the herbs used for contraceptive purposes, and for morning-after abortive purposes, was called *silphium* and was discovered by the Greeks at a place called Cyrene on the coast of what is now Libya. The unfortunately-named Soranus recommended adding a pea-sized measure of liquid from the plant to water once a month since "it not only prevents conception but also destroys anything existing". The Roman poet Catullus, musing how many kisses he and his girl-friend Lesbia might enjoy, answers "as many grains of sand as there are on Cyrene's *silphium* shores". Even then, in the century before Christ, the sand must have been running low, for *silphium* was peculiarly native only to this stretch of Libyan coast and died out within the next century.

Other herbs recommended include *asafoetida*, which is from the same family as *silphium* but is also the secret ingredient in Worcestershire Sauce. So watch out next time you splash some of the latter into your Bloody Mary – you may be affecting your breeding prospects. Also used as contraceptives were Queen Anne's lace, pennyroyal, artemisia, myrrh and rue. Galen, born at the start of Hadrian's reign and subsequently the foremost Roman physician, recommended pomegranate seeds as a vaginal suppository.

The curious thing about all this is that modern science has shown that these herbs do work. Extracts of *asafoetida* used on rats prevented pregnancy three days after mating, Queen Anne's lace is known to block the production of progesterone, which is necessary in preparation of the uterus for a fertilized ovum, and pennyroyal was shown to contain a substance that terminated pregnancy. Not too sure about the pomegranate seeds, though. The jury's still out on that one but all in all it is clear that Roman women had significant control over their fertility.

We don't know which of these methods Sabina used, of course, though I quite like to fancy that she used the old pomegranate-seed method and that's why Hadrian got the pip with her. That's if she had the need to use anything at all, for the reasons for her distaste of her husband Hadrian may not have been down to his lack of physical charms.

Roman women, like women everywhere in the classical world, were second-class citizens generally. Their function was largely to look pretty in order to attract men and thus continue the species, so, even though they had significant freedom of movement, they spent a lot of their time titivating themselves to attract the menfolk. Clothing fashion curiously changed little over the centuries of the Roman Empire. Roman women, however, were not unaware of the sexual allure of materials like silk. Here's Seneca on the subject:

> *"There I see silken clothes, if they can be called clothes*
> *which protect neither a woman's body nor her modesty,*
> *and in which she cannot truthfully declare that she is*
> *not naked. These are bought for huge sums from na-*
> *tions unknown to us in the ordinary course of trade*
> *– and why? So that our women may show as much of*
> *themselves to the world as they show to their lovers in*
> *the bedroom."*

Then there was the jewellery. No self-respecting woman would be seen without a goodly display of jewels – bracelets, ear-rings, finger-rings, ankle-rings, hairpins, buckles, and any number of different brooches, all made in gold, silver or bronze. You can see quite a few examples of this in the various sites on the Wall. This bling-bling was not tiny stuff either. The Roman writer Petronius tells us of the millionaire Trimalchio's wife wearing gold amulets that weighed six pounds. And Emperor Caligula's consort was reputed to own jewels worth £400,000.

As for make-up and hairstyling, perhaps it would be best to let another Roman writer, Lucian, tell us:

> *"They beautify the ugly skin of their face with an*
> *array of cosmetics. As if at a public procession*
> *each maid carries something – a silver jar, a bot-*
> *tle, a mirror, or a chemist's shop of little jars, all*
> *vials of abomination, treasures to polish the teeth*
> *or blacken the eyebrows and lashes. But most time*
> *and energy is spent on curling the hair. This lady*
> *dips her hair in henna to redden it and dries it in*
> *the midday sun like some wool-dyer, because she*
> *despises its natural colour. That lady thinks black*
> *hair suits her, so she spends all her husband's mon-*
> *ey on it; all the perfumes of Arabia sweeten her lit-*
> *tle hair. With steel tongs heated in the fire's gentle*
> *flame, she forces her curls into shape. In front she*
> *carries them carefully down to her eyebrows, so*

that only a small space of brow is left, while be-
hind, her curls fall and ripple coquettishly."

Other women dyed their hair blonde with yellow soap, while some wore wigs made from the hair of captive barbarians. Hair was frequently worn very high in elaborate braids or curls, sometimes arranged on crescent-shaped wire frames. Sabina, however shrewish she might have been in Hadrian's eyes, would certainly have followed the fashion of her peers in wearing jewellery, in painting make-up on her eyebrows and eyelashes, in whitening her teeth, in dabbing perfume on herself, in curling her hair, and generally seeking to enhance whatever natural beauty she possessed with the aid of cosmetics.

Roman men, on the other hand, were less fastidious, although we can notice fashions in hair styles in the busts of emperors that have been preserved. We know that Julius Caesar was almost bald, for instance, and that he was the first man in history who sought to hide that baldness with a comb-over, although in his case it was strictly speaking a comb-forward as he insisted on wearing the few remaining strands of his hair pulled forward over his brow. That was why he preferred to be seen wearing a wreath on his head, to hide the extensive bald pate. Nero, by way of contrast, had his hair set in long rows of curls and let it grow down his back. Hadrian too has his hair in curls in all the statues and busts that have come down to us, such as the one in the British Museum.

But Hadrian introduced a new trend to the men of the Roman Empire – the beard. Shaving with razors had been going on in various parts of the world for the best part of 3,000 years but, ever since Alexander had become obsessive about not going into battle with a five o'clock shadow, it had become normal for men to be clean-shaven. Roman males would start their day with a trip to the barber's for a shave, a chat about the recent gladiatorial games and to hear the latest dirty jokes.

The shaving was done with a thin-bladed iron razor, introduced to Rome by Sicilian barbers who would later use their instruments to take out *mafioso* contracts. So popular was shaving, in fact, that, when young men aged about twenty-one were having their first shave, this was witnessed by a gang of their mates who would turn up and party – only trainee philosophers were excused this ritual apparently, so no party for you, Umberto Eco, or for you, Thomas Aquinas. But, when Hadrian became emperor in A.D. 118, already sporting a beard officially in honour of his love for all things Greek but really because he had a bit of a spotty face, suddenly shaving became unpopular and Roman males began to sport hairy chins.

Roman women believed they were more sexually alluring without bodily hair, which is why you never see a statue of a Roman woman sporting pubic or underarm hair. They depilated like crazy, using creams with weird ingredients such as resin, pitch, white vine or ivy gum extract, ass's fat, she-goat's gall, bat's blood, and powdered viper. Such depilation was practiced by homosexual males as well, who also washed their faces in asses' milk to keep them fresh. Here's the Roman writer Martial on the latter:

> *"You depilate your arms, your legs, your bosom,*
> *And shave yourself, even your hairy loins.*
> *Of course you do it for your mistress, don't you?*
> *Still, others might have your smooth end in view."*

And it's at this point that I really need to tell you why Sabina was not overfond of her husband, for the great love of Hadrian's life was another male, named Antinous.

Antinous was born in the town of Claudiopolis, in the Greek province of Bithynia in what is now Turkey, around A.D. 110. He may have become part of Hadrian's court as a young boy, where he would have joined other young boys in the training school preparing them for services to the Emperor – services which could equally well be servicing as serving, for this was actually a harem of young boys. Homosexuality between older men and young boys was a normal feature of the classical world, much recommended by the Greeks, so we shouldn't be shocked by it even in our enlightened times. As long as the older man was the inserter, that is in the superior power position, he was okay – a proper man, in other words. In the old Grecian way, the love of a man for a boy was considered to be the purest form of love. Love for a woman, ancient philosophers held, was wasteful, for a woman was an inferior being and lust felt for a woman was a dirty thing, only necessary for producing sprogs. But a boy was equal in all ways except age and hence worthy of adoration. In return for providing respect, devotion and sexual gratification to the older man, the young boy would receive training in mind, body, morals and customs, as well as devoted affection. Well, that was their excuse.

It's possible that Hadrian encountered Antinous for the first time on his travels in Bithynia and brought him into his court at that point. By all accounts he was a beautiful hunk with a sharp mind and considerable intelligence. He was also reputed to be a good hunter, and hunting was one of Hadrian's great passions. It seems likely that he became Hadrian's favourite somewhere between A.D. 123 and 128, just as he was entering puberty, for we know that Antinous accompanied the Emperor on his trip to Greece in that latter year. But Antinous was more than just a favourite, more than the Emperor's passing fancy of the moment. Hadrian clearly became besotted with him, which is why the mystery of the young man's death holds an eternal fascination for us.

In A.D. 130 Hadrian embarked on a journey to Egypt with Antinous among his courtiers. While there the emperor rebuilt Pompey's tomb, probably visited the tomb of Alexander the Great, had some philosophical arguments with Egyptian scholars (he always fancied himself as a bit of a superbrain did Hadrian), and took his young lover on a lion-hunt in the desert. Then the entourage set sail up the Nile, passing through Heliopolis, Memphis, and Oxyrrhynchus till they reached Hermopolis where the mystery begins. For here, we are told, Antinous drowned, either after falling in the water, as Hadrian himself claimed, or by being offered in sacrifice, as some of his more unkind critics alleged.

Now you wouldn't easily make a sacrifice, literally, of someone you loved deeply, would you? And Hadrian's subsequent actions showed that his love for the Bithynian youth was unparallelled and unquestionable. On the other hand, Hadrian, like all Romans, was deeply superstitious and was constantly checking out the auspices in his Daily Male (sorry!) and would have known that this was the anniversary of the drowning of the Egyptian god Osiris. Maybe Antinous, who was reputedly pretty bright, knew about this too and, rather than being pushed, actually jumped into the Nile, offering himself as a sacrifice. Who knows?

What we do know is that Hadrian was griefstricken at the death of his young favourite, and contemporary writers believed that he remained in mourning for the rest of his life. On the opposite bank of the Nile from Hermopolis, he founded a city and called it Antinopolis. A new star was discovered shortly after Antinous's death and given his name in the theory that it was his soul shining down on Earth. Wherever he went, Hadrian ordered statues to be built of his young lover who had so tragically died and Antinous was actually deified and duly worshipped.

Now this all sounds a bit Princess Di really, doesn't it? Apparently there are worshippers who turn up regularly at the shrine to the late princess in Althorp Park, bearing gifts of gold, frankincense and myrrh, wreathing her tomb in gorgeous arrays of flowers, and generally venerating her as if she were some latter-day goddess. It's all Tony Blair's fault, isn't it? Ever since, on the morning after she died, he labelled her "the People's Princess", she's been turned into this semi-religious icon. It wouldn't surprise me if there wasn't already some bunch of nutters calling themselves something like The Society for the Worship of Diaphanous Diana and worshipping her blessed memory in some bizarre ways, like sporting Gucci dresses for breakfast or wearing six inch-long eyelashes.

So we shouldn't be too sniffy about the way that Hadrian turned his young lover into a god to be worshipped nor should we be too surprised that large parts of the Roman Empire joined in the adulation. After all, the Roman world had its media manipulators just as ours does. They even had schools to train blokes in spin doctoring, except they called it rhetoric, and it was considered a right-on sort of thing to be good at. In fact, under the Romans training in rhetoric became the major feature of the educational system. Being able to persuade others that black was white became the way to claim status in Roman society. Oodles of handbooks were published and special schools were set up. Top orators, in fact, could earn a fortune. Yes, spin-doctoring was all the rage in Rome. Word of mouth, when it seems to come from a high-ranking source, is just as powerful whether it comes as verbal gossip or as newspaper headlines.

And as for the differing versions of Antinous's death and whether it was accident, sacrifice or suicide, just remember the conspiracy theories about Princess Di's death. Was it really an accident? Or had Prince Philip organised a hit squad? Was the crown scared of the possibility of her marrying the Moslem Dodi Fayed? Was the Queen anxious that Di was pregnant and that an offspring with a possible claim to the throne, and incidentally head of the Church of England, might be a Muslim?

And how many films and books have there been about Jack Kennedy's death? We all know about the grassy knoll, the bookstore, the open-top car, the number of bullets fired, Lee Harvey Oswald's Russian wife and all the rest of it, even though few of us have ever been to Dallas and many were not even alive when it happened. So it would have been in the ancient Roman world. The unexpected death of the high and mighty shocks us all and we all want to seek explanations through the prism of our own beliefs.

That's why I believe that Antinous, Princess Di and President Kennedy were all killed on the secret orders of the Ancient Guild of Conspiracy Theorists. Well? It keeps them in work, doesn't it?

VII
Hoofing to Housesteads /
Veering to Vindolanda

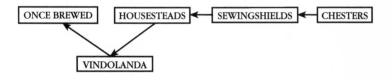

"I don't know who's going to do it when we give up," said Sandra Maughan the next morning as she was bringing our breakfasts. "They're depending on all us older folk but there's no youngsters taking on the farms nowadays who'll want to do it."

She was talking about the shortage of accommodation in this central area of the Hadrian's Wall Path. You are warned that you need to book in advance because of this shortage and it's not just because there's not enough people willing to set up in the B&B business; it's because the land is scarcely populated in this bleak part of the north.

"We all know each other up here," Sandra continued. "If I'm full, I know who else might put people up. Some of them's not in the official books but they've mebbe got a spare room, ye know."

"When's your busiest time?" asked Ben, one of my three Canadian fellow-guests at Green Carts Farm.

"Ooh, we get people all through the year," she answered, bringing out more toast and coffee. "I've had all sorts here, ye know. I had the Time Team, ye know, that Tony Robinson."

The Canadians smiled but clearly didn't know what she meant. I explained about the former Baldrick and his current TV persona heading up this team of suitably eccentric-looking archaeologists to survey famous sites in Britain.

"There was this American whose rucksack was full of books – it must have killed him to walk with that lot. Then there was this chap who was riding along the Wall on horseback on a wooden saddle. I don't know what he was trying to prove," she smiled. "I had these two seventy-five-year-olds call in last week. They were driving along the Wall to check out that they could get comfy accommodation."

"I have to say they couldn't ask for better than here," said Diane, one of the two Canadian women.

"Mind you, some of them can be a bit picky about our water," Sandra went on with a wry grin. "We've got our own bore hole, ye see. The water's got no chlorine and it's got bugs. But they're our bugs. Some people need their chemicals."

And with that she retreated to the kitchen, leaving the Canadians looking aghast at each other and me smiling to myself.

Sandra is one of these typical northerly women, hewn from the local stone, strong, fearless and gentle simultaneously. You could be mistaken on first meeting her to think she was a woman of less complexity than she is but, as you engage in conversation and reflect on what she is conveying, you realise she has a sharp perception of human beings and is not taken in by the flummery of the day. I felt privileged to be watched over by her.

Bidding fond farewells, I left Sandra Maughan at her kitchen door and set off through the chicken-filled farmyard back in the direction of the Wall. Within minutes I was at Black Carts Turret situated on another long stretch of surviving Wall, such as I was to come across frequently on this, my third day's walking. It was curious to find this stretch of the Wall, nearly 2000 years old, for no apparent reason just standing in the middle of a green field where cows munched contentedly.

There was a strongish westerly breeze blowing which gave a nice fresh feel to the early morning and it felt good to be walking into it. It wasn't long before I came up a hill to the site of Brocolitia Fort at Carrawburgh, where a metal notice at the edge of a car park, signed by R. Du Cane, Freeholder, tells you that it was occupied successively between A.D. 134 and 383 by garrisons of Aquitanians from southern France, and Cugernians and Batavians from Germany. There's not much to be seen of the fort nowadays, though the ramparts are visible, so it's a bit of a mystery why R. Du Cane, who may have been left behind by his Aquitanian forebears, should be warning you to keep your dog on a lead, but a short path takes you downhill into some boggy ground where in 1949 the remains of a Mithraic temple were found. It's a curious place now because what you see is a reconstruction of the three altars that were found and the gnome-like figures of Cautes and Cautopates, the originals being in Newcastle Museum of Antiquities.

Nearby is Coventina's Well, which had been dedicated to the local Celtic water goddess. Here a huge hoard of some 13,487 Roman coins was discovered by John Clayton in 1876. He also found a load of other objects like jars, pearls, brooches, incense burners, photographs of Pavarotti and Tony Bennett CDs but we don't need to go into all that. It was the coins find that was the best – four gold ones, 184 silver ones and the remainder bronze. Some of them are dated to the time of Emperor Antoninus Pius, who succeeded Hadrian and drove north to create the Antonine Wall between the Forth and the Clyde; others are dated to Hadrian himself. Many are on display in the Chesters Museum. Unfortunately, there are not as many available for scrutiny as Clayton discovered, because, when word spread of his discovery in the days following, the locals snuck in at night and half-inched a load of them.

After Brocolitia, there's a longish stretch when you're still following the line of the Military Road, mostly in or along the forward ditch. All this time you're climbing but it's a great relief when the Military Road finally veers off to the south, following the line of the Vallum but south of it, and the Path sticks closely to the line of Wall itself. There's lots of Wall, plus the remains of milecastles, as you approach Sewingshields Crags, where there is a farmhouse made entirely from stones off the Wall.

On this site once stood Sewingshields Castle, where local legend tells that King Arthur and Queen Guinevere held court. One day, being bored with life in general, Arthur, Guinevere, Merlin et al were playing Squabble in the Great Hall on the Round Table. Merlin, who was getting a bit ancient and was losing his marbles, missed a big score, and when he realised this, he cursed. Unfortunately, his curse was an ancient one and he got the words the wrong way round, with the result that everyone present was turned into silent statues. Allegedly they are still underground in a huge enchanted cavern waiting until the British nation calls on their help. Beside them, on a table, sit a horn, a sheathed sword and a garter. To awaken the great King, so the legend goes, someone must draw the sword, cut the garter and blow the horn.

Apparently some Northumbrian farmer was sitting on the rocks above knitting (that's when you know this is a dodgy story – a farmer knitting?) when his ball of wool fell through a crack in the rocks. Squeezing himself through the crack, the farmer found himself in the underground vault and there were Arthur and his gang, sleeping just as legend foretold. The farmer took the sword and cut the garter but forgot to blow the horn. Arthur awoke for long enough to utter these immortal words:

O Woe betide that evil day
On which this witless wight was born,
Who drew the sword, the garter cut,
But never blew the bugle-horn.

Then Arthur went back to sleep. He apparently always spoke in verse, even when he was only awake for a few seconds.

One of the ironies of this story is that a film released in 2005, entitled *King Arthur*, portrays Arthur as a dissatisfied Roman warrior left behind on Hadrian's Wall when the Roman army cleared off at the start of the 5th century. According to this film, he was just a mercenary soldier, not the great hero of romance, and he lived in Northumbria, not in Cornwall or even Wales which have previously claimed him. Did someone know of Sewingshields Crags? Had someone really found the sleeping monarch and blown his bugle? I think not. And just to ensure that your illusions are totally smashed, I am pleased to inform you that the Hadrian's Wall featured in the film is not the original but was specially built for the occasion – in Ireland, where the filming took place.

From the high vantage point at Sewingshields, however, being careful not to let your ball of wool slip through any cracks in the rocks, you can see the vast Kielder Forest to the north and more closely the expanse of Broomlee Lough, while the Vallum marches along to the south much further away from the Wall than it has been so far, because of the geographical lie of the land.

Then it's back along remnants of the Wall again, up and down, as it follows the contours of the land. One of the dips between the hills is called Busy Gap, where a drovers' road once passed through. This was known as a place where the Jocks used to break through and harass the Roman army and later it became a well-known passing place for the Moss Troopers, of whom William Hutton reported:

> *"They could pass over bogs which nobody else could.*
> *They burrowed into rocks and holes which none could*
> *find out, and places where none durst approach."*

The Moss Troopers were bands of thieves and brigands living

in the borderlands which continued to produce its fair share of problems long after the Roman army had left. Here's how a 16th-century gent described them in a letter to his son:

> *"Ye shall perceive that on Saint James' Day even, the 24 July came Liddisdale men to the barony of Langley to the number of six score, and laid them at 'Buisy Yappe'; and sent forth 7 men and seized six oxen."*

The local bigwigs with menservants in tow set off in pursuit, unaware of the danger from the larger force of Moss Troopers awaiting them at Busy Gap.

> *"And our men wist the Scots brake upon them, and took them all both horse & man saving two persons: so the Scots rode in haste with their prisoners. Son, if there be no remedy for Liddesdale the country is in a schroved point, and true men that is oppressed for fear of their life and lossing of their goods say plainly that they will leave the country."*

Stand still at Busy Gap and you'll hear the snorting of their ponies and the quiet thud of the Moss Troopers' heels against the ponies' sides; you'll feel the air when it goes suddenly stale as their ghostly troop rushes past you; and you'll shiver at the thought that they've ignored you to press on to some better source of pillage.

Around the bend of one of these climbs I suddenly came upon a young woman sketching, so I stopped to admire her work. Her name was Karen Neale and she told me that she had taken extended leave from her firm of architects in London in order to undertake a commission gained through the Hadrian's Wall Partnership. This involved her in leading painting workshops in local communities along the Wall as a sort of outreach work. At the same time she was busy creating a record of her own journey along the Wall, west to east, by doing water paintings of scenes that attracted her. It was very breezy up there and Karen was well wrapped up but still complaining of the cold, so we arranged to meet for lunch at the nearby Housesteads Fort when she had completed her morning's work.

Housesteads Fort, or Vercovicium to give it its proper Roman name, is the place that probably gets the greatest number of visitors to Hadrian's Wall. There's nothing new about this. Housesteads has been drawing visitors since 1725 and William Hutton on his 1801 visit described it thus:

> *"I retreated next morning over a Moss to my favourite pursuit, which brought me to Housesteads, the grandest Station in the whole line. In some Stations the Antiquary feeds upon shells, but here upon kernels. Here lie the remains of ancient splendour in bold characters."*

Clearly, many of the buildings on the site of Vercovicium were still visible then, at least to some extent, before John Clayton bought Housesteads Farm and set about excavating it in 1838.

You really need to enter the fort remains through the east gate, as I did, because that way you can see what's left of the *principia* (headquarters) building, which was the administrative centre of the fort. The biggest space within the *principia* building was the central hall, at one end of which the fort's commanding officer would sit on ceremonial or public occasions. Here he would receive important visitors formally, or sit in judgment over some military misdemeanour, like some soldier being late on guard duty or scratching his bottom on parade. Other rooms in the building housed the garrison's flags and a shrine.

As you stroll around the Housesteads site, you can imagine yourself in a living, thriving fort, because it has virtually all been uncovered. So you know you are walking down streets where soldiers would have strolled, arguing the toss about whose turn it was to do the washing up, or centurions would have marched, chests puffed out to demonstrate their self-importance, or woad-encrusted Jocks would have been dragged in chains to their prison cells and probable death.

Perhaps the most telling edifice that reminds you of our common humanity with these Roman soldiers is the latrine building. In some ways this is the most famous building on the Wall, because what has been uncovered is so remarkably well preserved. You can see the water channels that the soldiers washed their sponges in after wiping their bottoms and the sewers which flushed everything away. Visiting the lavatory was a communal thing for the Roman soldiers, and a helpful diagram shows how the wooden seating would have been arranged along two walls above the sewers and the water channels.

"Hey, Cyn, look at this," a very big, red-faced man called out to his equally large female companion in an American drawl.

He was sporting a red baseball cap and one of those multi-coloured Hawaian beach shirts that I thought had gone out of fashion with Burt Reynolds.

"It's the Roman bathroom. I'm gonna try it. Get the camera out."

And with one bound, as they say – though in truth it was more like a giant jellyfish flopping – and ignoring the Keep Out signs, he was squatting over the trench where the wooden seating would have been.

"Can you move this way a bit, Jake?" cooed Cyn, whom I had already christened 'Deadly', as she pointed the video camera at Jake, holding his image as steady as she could in the viewfinder.

"Like here?" queried Jake, who had moved a couple of feet

closer to her.

"Yeah, that's t'rific," responded Deadly Cyn. "Just strain a bit."

"Gimme that stick," said Jake, grimacing in obedience to her command. "Pretend it's my sponge."

And he took the twig she picked up off the ground and thrust it vigorously up and down, simulating how he imagined the soldiers would have cleaned themselves after using the latrine.

"Great," said Deadly Cyn. "I got some real good pictures here. They'll love this back in Arkansaw."

I have always loved Americans for their subtlety.

The information centre and museum at Housesteads is helpful if you want a fuller picture, though the museum does not have anywhere near as much stuff as Chesters. Housesteads was occupied by auxiliary troops called the Tungrians from Belgium in the 3rd and 4th centuries, and I went for another stroll through those ghostly streets of the fort, imagining life on the Wall for those Belgian soldiers. Then I went downhill to the car park with its café where I met up with Karen Neale for an enjoyable luncheon, though sadly without any beer.

This central section of the Roman Wall is truly one of the most spectacular, as you follow what seems like miles of existing Wall swooping up and down the crags which bear lovely names like Cuddy's, Hotbank and Highshields. The Wall doesn't have the straight-lineness that you have come to expect from earlier manifestations, but the Roman engineers sensibly chose to follow the contours of the crags hereabouts. As you leave Housesteads you are actually walking on top of a short section of the Wall – the only bit you can now securely walk on because of understandable anxieties about its preservation. From atop you can see why Hadrian chose to build his defensive line on this natural escarpment, for it towers over the lands below and gives fantastic views out into the barren country to the north. The crags themselves would have been sufficiently offputting to the Jocks but a 14-foot Wall on top of it, patrolled by Roman soldiers, must have given even more reasons for retreating to Glasgow for some deep-fried Mars Bars and a wee nip or two of Irn Bru.

Just past Cuddy's Crags, the Hadrian's Wall Path becomes one with the Pennine Way, which was the first long-distance footpath in the United Kingdom. The Pennine Way stretches along the broad backbone of England from Edale in the south to Kirk Yetholm just across the border into Scotland. Many years ago it was traversed and described by Alfred Wainwright, the doyen of Lake District hill writers, and I have it in mind to tackle it to celebrate my 65th birthday, so I will say no more about it here.

Another equally fascinating landmark in a dip between two rises is what has come to be known as Sycamore Gap, where a lone sycamore planted itself some 80 years ago. In 1989 the National Trust, which cared for this part of the Wall, decided that the tree was nearing the end of its days, so they planted a sycamore sapling next to it, intending that this would replace the original when the latter died. The old tree, however, refused to die and, when the producers of the Kevin Costner film *Robin Hood, Prince of Thieves* decided to use Sycamore Gap for the opening shots of their film, they were faced with the problem of having two trees when, for dramatic effect, they only wanted the one sturdy example. So they built a shack around the sapling and made this the home of a simple lad whom Robin Hood was to rescue from the clutches of the wicked Sheriff of Nottingham (also holidaying in Northumberland at the time). The plot involved the shack going up in flames, which attracts Robin's attention and leads to a punch-up between the Merrie Men and the Sheriff's Unmerrie Men with the inevitable result. Sadly the sycamore sapling was damaged in the fire and has barely grown since.

Meanwhile the older tree continues to flourish. Is there a moral somewhere in there?

I walked at quite a lick that afternoon because I had planned to visit Vindolanda Fort, which is south of the Wall, but was staying at Gibbs Farm to the north. I knew that my only chance of doing this in time was to catch the A.D. 122. This is the imaginatively numbered (after the year of Hadrian's visit to initiate the building of the Wall), blue-and-white liveried, single-decker bus that plies its trade in the summer months along the length of the Wall from Wallsend to Bowness. It is a brilliant idea, really helpful to walkers who only want to do a short stretch of the Wall at a time and a valuable time-saver for me that Monday afternoon. I sped downhill from Steel Rigg towards the Twice Brewed Inn, because I saw a coach parked there and, although my watch told me it was too early for the A.D. 122, I was not entirely convinced that either my watch or the timetable I'd read at Housesteads was accurate.

I had nothing to fear. The coach was waiting at the Twice Brewed Inn. Slightly out of breath I waited patiently at the bus stop for the A.D. 122 outside the Visitors' Centre nearby at Once Brewed, and at exactly 14.38, the bus, with Spartacus inscribed on its front for some curious reason (he was a slave of a very different water), pulled up and on I got. Macho Wall walkers might consider this to be cheating but I was off the Wall, literally, and using A.D. 122 gave me an extra hour at the very wonderful Vindolanda Fort.

It's impossible to write about Vindolanda without mentioning the name Birley, the family that has been associated with it for over 70 years since Eric Birley, then a young archaeology lecturer at Durham University, my *alma mater*, purchased it. Eric Birley was one of the great enthusiasts who helped to develop Hadrian's Wall as a visitor attraction. The official guides for Corbridge,

Chesters and Housesteads still bear his name as their writer and he encouraged generations of young archaeologists to develop their trade through his work at Durham. Vindolanda is now run by a Trust but its development has been overseen by Eric Birley's son Robin, an eminent archaeologist in his own right; Robin's son Andrew is the new kid on the Wall, responsible for many of the latest developments at Vindolanda. Robin's brother Anthony, another distinguished academic, has written the definitive modern biography of Hadrian.

Vindolanda is the jewel in the crown on Hadrian's Wall, which is odd since it is actually a mile or so south of the Wall on the Stanegate connecting Carlisle and Corbridge. Built originally by Agricola's troops when the Stanegate was created, it was a supply fort for most of its existence. Like Corstopitum, it consequently developed a fairly large civil settlement around its perimeter, drawn there by the opportunities to service the fort's needs, whether those be manual, commercial or sexual.

The excavated layout of the fort – and, fascinatingly, it is still being excavated, for there were young people working during my visit – is like all the others. There's the typical playing card shape and there's the remains of the *principia* (headquarters) building, of the bath house – a particularly good one, I must admit, showing the underground heating system wonderfully well - the latrines, and the *mansio* (inn) for travellers. There are also superb replicas of the actual Wall itself, or rather of two bits of the Wall – a 25-yard section of the turf Wall, with wooden rampart and walkway, and a 15-yard section of stone Wall, complete with crenellations and a turret. These give you a real feel for the size of the construction which stretched 80 miles from coast to coast.

But you'll forgive me if I don't spend time on the buildings of the fort itself, because what the Birleys and their fellow-diggers have uncovered here is much more revealing about the lives of the Roman soldiers than you'll see anywhere else.

By an accident of nature, a part of the Vindolanda site stands on particularly boggy ground and it was here that Robin Birley made the discoveries that were to shake up thinking about Roman Britain. For here, in 1973, he uncovered the first written Roman documents ever to be found in Britain. The boggy ground had preserved these fragments of bark, with indistinct Latin writing on them, for almost 2000 years. It was a discovery of major importance which Birley describes thus:

> *"If I have to spend the rest of my life working in dirty, wet trenches, I doubt whether I shall ever again experience the shock and excitement I felt at my first glimpse of ink hieroglyphics on tiny scraps of wood."*

Since then, hundreds more pieces of wood have been uncovered in the same area. For example, the charred remains of some 300 writing tablets were found outside the commandant's house of what is believed to have been a bonfire dating to the period before Hadrian arrived. Vindolanda at that time was garrisoned by the Batavorum troops from Holland and, because of the dedicated work of teams of epigraphists, a picture has emerged of the men and women who lived here.

Thanks to these findings, the names of over 200 inhabitants of the fort have come down to us. These were the writers or recipients of letters or people referred to in letters or in lists of various kinds. For instance, there are letters to and from Neratius Marcellus, who we know was governor of Britain in A.D. 103 and who was a pal of the Roman writer Pliny. There's a fragment of another letter which mentions the receipt of underpants and socks, showing that the soldiers up north certainly felt the cold and welcomed extra clothing from Markus & Sparkus to supplement their uniform. There are lots of other pieces, revealing every strata of society at the camp, from slaves at the bottom to the commandant's wife at the top. One of the most interesting, because its humanity crosses the centuries, is an invitation to Lepidina, wife of the commandant Cerialis, to attend a birthday party of her friend Severa. There are lists of foodstuffs, which give us an insight into the dining habits of the troops, references to travelling expenses for journeys to York and to Rome, accounts of working parties at the fort and so much more.

To get some feel of the people revealed in these tablets, read the following complete letter from a man called Chrauttius to his messmate Veldeius:

> *"And I ask you, brother Veldeius – I am surprised that you have not written anything back to me for such a long time – whether you have heard anything from our kinsmen, or about Quotus – in which unit he is – and you are to greet him in my own words – and Virilis the vet. You are to ask him whether you may send through one of our people the shears which he promised me for a price. And I ask you, brother Virilis, that you greet from me sister Thuttena and write back to us about Velbuteius, how he is. I wish you may be very happy. Farewell."*

He sounds a bit negative, doesn't he? In fact he sounds a right old Sour Chrauttius, but you could picture him nowadays, couldn't you? It could even be you, dear gentle reader.

The Vindolanda museum has copies of some of these pieces of writing on display – the originals are obviously stored in appropriate conditions at the British Museum – among a whole host of other fascinating findings from the excavations. There's a wonderful array of sandals, for instance, looking like the sort of thing that Spiderman might wear, and various hobnailed shoes. There are bone counters together with a dice box and dice; a helpful inscription tells you that the dice is loaded and the six comes up eight times out of ten. There's a ladies' wig made out of locally-grown moss, which it is believed would have been worn to deter the midges.

It's altogether brilliant and, if you only have time to visit one site in Hadrian's Wall country, it has to be Vindolanda. Okay, the fort may not be as clearly excavated as at Housesteads and there's not the same sense of order that there is at Corbridge. But if you really want to get a feel of what these people were like who guarded the Northern frontier of the mighty Roman Empire, then Vindolanda's your man. There's even a description, the only one I can find anywhere, from one of the tablets, of the native Brits who were on the other side of the Wall and were the reason why Hadrian built the thing in the first place:

> *"...the Britons are unprotected by armour. There are very many cavalry. The cavalry do not use swords, nor do the wretched Britons mount in order to throw javelins."*

After touring the site and the museum, I paused for tea and carrot cake in the appropriately-named Café Lepidina, when my peace and quiet were interrupted by none other than Jake and Cyn, the American couple I had seen earlier that day at Housesteads.

"Whadda ya make of that bit of Wall then, Jakey?" Deadly Cyn queried. "Cute, eh?"

"Yeah," Jake answered, removing his baseball cap to reveal a thick red ridge at the top of his bald forehead. "Sure was. Hey, didn't we see ya at Housesteads?"

They, or rather Jake, had spotted me as they stood at the counter awaiting their coffee and cakes, for one slice each of carrot cake was insufficient for them to maintain their bodily grossness.

"Hi," I waved feebly back at them.

"Mind if we join ya?" continued Jake, moving to sit down at my table before I could respond. "We got nothing like this back home, y'know. Folks'll be real interested in what we seen."

"Whadda ya think of them Romans, eh?" asked Deadly, as she squeezed her large backside on to one of the delicate chairs in the café, needing to force the table out a couple of feet in order to do so. "Amazing people, weren't they? I love that story about how they beat Boudeka."

That was it. I wasn't going to take this any longer.

"Listen," I said, tossing my head back in the way you're supposed to in such moments of high drama. "Her name was Boadicea, not Boudeka."

I stood up to leave.

"Have a nice day," I finished, admittedly in a rather feeble fashion but I felt I'd made my point.

And I stalked out, to the imaginary cheers of several thousand of my Pictish forebears, who would dearly have loved to have treated their Roman overlords in the same fashion.

I felt elated as I left Vindolanda, and not just because of my little victory over Jake and Deadly. It was 20 years since I'd last been there and I recalled that as a memorable experience. It has got better and better since then, to the extent that I almost wished I had continued with my classical education, so I could join in the deciphering of those tiny fragments of writing. Entertaining such thoughts almost made me miss the A.D. 122 back to Once Brewed, from where I had a couple of miles to go to reach Gibbs Farm.

First though, I had to stop to quench my thirst at the Twice Brewed Inn. Legend has it that the pub is called this because General "Virginia" Wade, on his way to Carlisle to intercept Bonnie Prince Charlie, called there for a pint of best and, not being satisfied with the strength of the beer, ordered that it should be brewed again. The result was so good that Wade overstayed his time and, by the time he reached Carlisle, the Bonnie Prince had gone. Hence the pub became the Twice Brewed Inn. As for Once Brewed, this is the name of the youth hostel, which was opened in 1934 by a certain Lady Trevelyan who was a committed teetotaller. Noticing that the Twice Brewed Inn was uncomfortably close, she announced, "We will serve nothing stronger than tea and I hope even that will only be once brewed."

I refreshed myself with a couple of pints of Twice Brewed bitter, which the landlord told me was really Yates's best bitter, brewed in Aspatria in Cumbria, but rebadged specially for the pub. It was very tasty, though I could also have had Fortis stout, brewed even nearer at Bardon Mill. The inn was almost empty, though I gathered this was unusual, as it is virtually the only refreshment stop for miles around. It's a most atmospheric place and I had hoped to spend the night there, but when I had telephoned two months beforehand, it was already fully booked, such is the demand for accommodation in the central section of the Wall.

So off I trudged for the final part of my day's walk to Gibbs Farm in the valleys beyond the crags that carry the Roman Wall, where I received a lovely warm welcome from its owner Val Gibson and where later that evening I dined contentedly before retiring.

VIII

HADRIAN THE SPORTSMAN

One thing we know for sure about Hadrian was that he was a keen hunter. What he would have hunted, in general, would have been mostly deer and wild boars, though he would also have had opportunities in some parts of the Roman Empire for hunting more exotic animals like bears or lions. Less dangerous sport would have been snaring hares or wildfowl. But it was in the excitement of the chase that Hadrian would have been following a long tradition among the Roman ruling class, charging round the countryside shouting the Latin equivalent of 'Tally ho!'. Whether he hunted in Britain on his visit we do not know, though, since he was travelling the length of his proposed Wall, it is conceivable that he would have taken advantage of the opportunities provided by this stretch of Britain. Did he discover here the joys of hunting with dogs? It is possible, since several writers refer to dogs being specifically bred for hunting by the natives of Britain. These dogs might well have been from a breed known as Agassian, which were small, squat and thin but with powerful claws and wicked teeth. These dogs were in big demand on mainland Europe and were exported from Celtic Britain.

Hadrian began hunting as a teenager while he was staying in his family's home town of Italica. Spain in those days was home to wild boars, stags and wild goats, providing plenty of opportunity for a young man armed with a spear and a fast horse to develop his expertise in the hunt. In fact, apparently Hadrian threw himself into his sporting life so thoroughly that his guardian Trajan had to bring him back to Rome to remind him of his other duties.

We are all reasonably familiar with the notion of hunting for deer, largely, I guess, from the stories of Robin Hood in the greenwood forests of Sherwood in Nottinghamshire (or Yorkshire or Northumberland, depending on your prejudice). But boar hunting? Can you imagine chasing a pig? Mind you, these were rather larger and fiercer than your average porker, being about three feet at the shoulders, five feet in total length, weighing about 200 pounds, and with two great long tusks. These were what Hadrian enjoyed hunting on his horse Borysthenes, after whose death the Emperor wrote this touching little poem:

> *Borysthenes Alanus,*
> *the swift horse of Caesar,*
> *who was accustomed to fly*
> *through the sea and the marshes*
> *and the Etruscan mounds,*
> *while pursuing Pannonian boars. Not one boar*
> *dared him to harm*
> *with his white tooth:*
> *the saliva from his mouth*
> *scattered even the meanest tail,*
> *as is the custom to happen.*
> *But killed on a day in his youth,*
> *his healthy, invulnerable body*
> *has been buried here in the field.*

Aren't you moved?

Curiously enough, there is now a growing number of boars at large in Britain, despite the well-attested fact that the last wild one was officially hunted down in 1617. Seemingly some that were kept in captivity escaped during violent storms in the 1980s and began to breed, so there are now something like 250 or so roaming freely in the Midlands and the South West. One was reported to have charged a woman on horseback in Ross-on-Wye in Herefordshire. No doubt she'll have been one of those trying to storm Parliament in recent times over the ban on fox-hunting.

We also know that Hadrian had at least one opportunity to hunt a lion, because there was a series of relief sculptures which recorded the emperor and Antinous engaged in just this activity in the Egyptian desert, shortly before the young man's death. According to legend, this lion had long terrorized the surrounding territory, roaring around as if it was in a Tarzan film, scavenging in the Egyptians' dustbins and eating their babies. It would therefore have been a suitable prey for the mighty emperor and his party. The story we're given is that Hadrian struck the fatal blows himself but then they would say that, wouldn't they? There's a long tradition of courtiers sucking up to their rulers by making out they had done something fantastically courageous, when in fact it was committed often by some lowly slaves.

Not satisfied with pursuing their beastly activities in the far-flung reaches of the Empire, the Romans brought hunting to the capital itself, holding hunts in the city stadia on the mornings before gladiatorial shows to entertain the punters. The hunters were criminals, chucked into the arenas with no weapons or protective armour to kill beasts or be killed. The animals came from all over the empire and included lions, elephants, bears, deer, wild goats, dogs, and camels. And this was no small-scale entertainment, believe me. The Romans were a bloodthirsty lot and thousands of animals would die in a single day. For instance, at the games held to celebrate Trajan's accession as Emperor, over 9,000 animals were killed.

Can you imagine that? What kind of a strike rate is that?

Thanks to Hollywood, we know all about the Roman games. Remember that scary chariot race in *Ben Hur* when Charlton Heston had to dodge the spikes on the wheels of his opponent's chariot? And can you ever forget Russell Crowe's glistening pecs in *Gladiator* as he faced his challenges in the gladiatorial arena?

The Roman poet Juvenal wrote of how the Roman people gave away their rights of self-determination to the emperors in return for *panem et circenses* (bread and circuses), by which he did not mean Billy Smart's big top, Coco the Clown and poodles dressed up as dolls. The Circus Maximus in Rome was the name given to the oval-shaped arena in which chariot racing took place. There were four famous Roman chariot stables, the Reds, the Whites, the Blues, and the Greens – a bit like Arsenal, Tottenham, Chelsea and Queens Park Rangers – and each had their special set of fans, who developed their own chants ("Come on, you Reds" being heard for the first time in Rome, not in Liverpool) and their own fan clubs. No doubt they also turned up to the chariot races stoned out of their heads on Valpolicella and wearing togas of the appropriate colour with the name of their *numero uno* charioteer stitched on the back.

The charioteers were originally slaves but, if they were good enough, they soon earned enough from their endeavours to buy their freedom, for there was a fortune at stake in these races, and huge amounts of betting in the crowds where 'Onest 'Oratio would offer dodgy odds to greedy punters. The charioteers wore precious little bodily protection, merely a light helmet. The top charioteers were massively popular – a piece of graffiti in Pompeii states "Celadus the Thracian makes the girls sigh" - and women allegedly wet their pants at the sight of their latest heart-throb. Presumably that's why the Emperor Nero fancied himself as a charioteer and even had an arena specially built for himself. Transfers between teams also took place: a charioteer named Diocles, for instance, drove for six years for the Whites (Tottenham), three years with the Greens (QPR) and fifteen years for the Reds (Arsenal).

The chariots were very small, being little more than a tiny platform on an axle, on which the charioteer had to stand, the reins wrapped dangerously round his waist as he sought to drive his four thoroughbred horses faster and faster around the circuit. Cheating was commonplace, both during the race and before it, as Ben Hur showed graphically. Attempts were made to poison the horses and/or the charioteers with spiked Asti Spumante before races, illegal braking systems would be used, shunting of opponents was common, and charioteers of German origin whose fathers made shoes usually won. Chariot-racing was very much the Formula One stuff of its day.

Although the charioteers got the glory, the real heroes were, naturally, the highly-trained horses of the four teams. The horses in the film *Ben Hur*, all 78 of them, were from Slovenia and were trained for months before filming began. So well trained were they, in fact, that when at the beginning of the chariot race Charlton Heston shook the reins, the four horses remained motionless. This went on a few minutes until someone from the camera crew shouted "Giddy-up", whereupon the horses charged off, flinging Heston backwards off the chariot.

Altogether now, aaah!

A tale is told of a charioteer who every day walked into the stable to exercise his horse, Julius. He would call out:

"Hey there, Julius, how's everything today?" and then bridle his horse.

One day while going through this routine he said, "Hey there, Julius...", when, to his surprise, the horse turned around and interrupted him.

"For months now, you've walked in here and said, 'Hey there, Julius, how's everything today?' and I'm tired of it. You never wait for an answer, and besides, my name is Marcus."

And with that, the horse ran off at speed.

Shocked, the charioteer took off after the horse trying to catch it. Seeing the pursuit, his dog joined the chase. After a while the man became tired and stopped to rest at the side of the road. He took out his handkerchief and wiped his face as his dog, who had continued the chase, came back also now breathless, and sat down beside him.

"I've never heard a horse talk before," the man said aloud to himself.

"Me neither," said the dog, gasping for air.

When George Orwell described professional sport as "War minus the shooting", he might well have been describing gladiatorial contests in Roman times, except that there was shooting, metaphorically at any rate, for the result of most contests was the death of one of the gladiators. Roman historians tried to claim that gladiatorial combat was a relic of religious ceremonies enacted by the Etruscans and the Greeks, but there is no doubt in my mind that the Roman enthusiasm for gladiatorial battle merely echoed their lust for world domination through their army. Allegedly, the first games were held in honour of a dead Roman aristocrat, but by Julius Caesar's time the gladiatorial games were a regular feature of life in Rome. So much so that Julius had a specially-built amphitheatre erected and organised for over 300 bouts to take place at any one time.

The gladiators were originally condemned criminals, prisoners of war, or slaves bought for the purpose of gladiatorial combat, though some in later days of the Roman Empire were free men seeking fame and fortune. They would attend specialist gladiator academies, where they would be trained in the use of weapons, such as the war chain, net, trident, dagger, and lasso. They would also receive a special diet and first-class medical attention, which no doubt included being given performance-enhancing drugs and being introduced to the magic sponge. The most famous of these academies was at Capua in Campania, from where the slave Spartacus (or Kirkus Douglus) escaped and raised an army against the Romans in 73 B.C. To prevent the possibility of this happening again the academies were later taken over as official state-run institutions.

The wannabe gladiators had to select from four different modes of armour and weaponry. You could be a common or garden Samnite, with a large oblong shield, a leather leg-guard on your left leg, a posh helmet with a crest and plume, and a glittering sword. You could be a Thracian, with a round shield, both legs protected by leather leg-guards, an open-faced helmet, and a curved sword. You could be a Secutor, with a large oval shield, a round helmet, leather bands round your elbows and wrists, and a short dagger or sword. Or – and this is the best of them – you could be a Retiarius, wearing only a loin-cloth and a metal shoulder-guard on your left arm, with a net, a dagger and a trident. There were a few variations. The Emperor Nero introduced women gladiators, but he would, wouldn't he? The Emperor Domitian pitted female gladiators against dwarves, but that's no surprise from that voluptuary either. There were also gladiators who fought blindfolded in helmets with no eyeholes. Others fought on horseback or from chariots, using lances and lassos as well as swords.

Gladiators were highly-trained, highly-prized, highly-regarded professional athletes, who only fought two or three times a year. If they survived three to five years, they could become free men, as Russell Crowe's Maximus aspired to be. Few did, for obvious reasons. If you thought that football managers have a short span in office, you should try being a gladiator. You get yourself into the peak of condition, your sword's newly sharpened, your helmet's polished until it looks like new, you've marched into the arena in procession to the cheers of the adoring crowd ("Beckum, Beckum, Beckum"), you've joined in the shout of "Those who are about to die salute you", you've got all the girls swooning over you in their seats in the Colosseum, and then they put you into a fight with that bastard with the net, the Retiarius. You never like fighting them and this one's trickier than most. Still, you keep him and his blasted trident at bay for what seems like ages and then you trip. Before you can say Jackus Robinsonus, his net is wrapped round you, his trident is lunging at you and there's blood coming out of your belly. You raise your left hand with your finger outstretched pleading for mercy but the crowd's not in a forgiving mood and they give you the old thumbs down treatment.

And that's it. The Retiarius raises his arm and, even though you're clinging to his leg and giving him the forlorn look, stabs you in the neck and kills you. No freedom for you, mate. No Roman girlies lifting up their tunics and offering you a glimpse of heaven. The attendants come on to drag your body off, one of them checking with a hot iron that you're not faking, and you're for the knackers' yard.

Imagine that happening on a Saturday afternoon somewhere, anywhere, in Britain. You can't, can you? We're much more civilised nowadays, of course. Our gladiatorial contests, our soccer matches, are played in a different spirit, where all concerned are careful to avoid even touching let alone injuring opposing players, aren't they?

I've pointed out earlier that the evidence of amphitheatres in Britain is thin, though it seems likely that the Roman soldiers would have wanted their sport just like modern-day squaddies do. It's probable therefore that there were gladiatorial contests in the country. Recent excavations in London found the body of a young woman buried with a number of items which indicate the strong possibility that she was a female gladiator. If that is so, then certainly there would have been gladiatorial contests elsewhere in the country. Were slaves brought from mainland Europe to fight here? Were the contestants captured Picts with their blue woad tattoos? Or was it the equivalent of going to a wrestling event in Carlisle nowadays, to see some clapped-out old farts wobbling through their pre-arranged jumps, grunts, pratfalls and braggadocio?

Since Trivial Pursuits had not yet been invented, Hadrian and his squaddies had to find other indoor games to occupy them on the dark nights up north. The Romans played a wide variety of board games, including *Tali & Tropa* (Knucklebones), *Tesserae* (Dice), *Latrunculi* (Roman Chess), *Calculi* (Roman Checkers), *Duodecim Scripta* (The Game of Twelve Lines), *Felix Sex* (The Game of Lucky Sixes), *Terni Lapilli* (Tic-Tac-Toe), *Tabula* (Roman Backgammon), and *Senet* (Egyptian Backgammon).

Felix Sex (which has nothing to do with a cat or sex) is a sort of precursor of Scrabble, though it looks fiendishly difficult. The experts aren't entirely sure but they think that the game board contained 36 letters, from which by throwing three dice you had to compose six words each of six letters. If you were really smart you could compose clever messages such as this:

VENARI	LAVARI
LUDERE	RIDERE
OCCEST	VIVERE

Which means "hunting, bathing, playing games and laughing, this is the life."

Or this:

LEVATE	DALOCU
LUDERE	NESCIS
IDIOTA	RECEDE

Which means "get up and leave, you don't know this game, idiot, quit."

Tabula was even more complicated, though, if you've ever had a go at backgammon, you'll be familiar with the basic pattern. The Chinese attribute the origins of backgammon to India and no doubt it reached Rome through its imperial expansion into the far east, though versions of backgammon developed all over the place at around the same time – Iceland, Egypt, England, Spain, You can still see old men playing backgammon in many parts of the world to this day, sitting at tables on street corners with pipes in their mouths, carpet slippers on their feet, and several days' stubble on their chins.

Here's how to play the Roman *tabula*, in case you want to be like those old men.

The Rules of Tabula

1. *The board can be a backgammon board. Each player has 15 pieces.*
2. *All pieces enter from square 1 and travel counterclockwise.*
3. *Three dice are thrown, and the three numbers deter mine the moves of between 1 and 3 pieces*
4. *Any part of a throw which cannot be used is lost, but a player must use the whole value of the throw if it is possible.*
5. *If a player lands a piece on a point with one enemy piece, the enemy piece is removed from the board and has to re-enter the game on the next throw.*
6. *If a player has 2 or more men on a point, this position is closed to the enemy, and these men cannot be captured.*
7. *No player may enter the second half of the board until all men have entered the board.*
8. *No player may exit the board until all pieces have entered the last quarter. This means that if a single man is hit, the remaining pieces may be frozen in the last quarter until he re-enters and catches up with them again.*

Got it? Good luck then. But if you find these two games all too challenging, you might prefer something more straightforward like *Orca*, which simply consisted of chucking seeds into a jar. Or maybe *Calculi* is more to your taste. Using a board with eight by eight squares, the object of the game is to get five of your colour in a row, taking alternate turns. A bit like Noughts and Crosses, isn't it?

We don't know Hadrian's game of choice, though we know that other Emperors indulged. Claudius, for example, was a dead keen gambler at *Tabula* – he even had his imperial carriage fitted out with a board so that he could play while he was swanning around the Empire. He also wrote a history of the game but sadly, for I know you'd love to be regaled by what I suppose would be the Roman equivalent of *Budgie the Magic Helicopter*, no copy of it has survived.

IX
Boogieing to Birdoswald /
Listing to Lanercost

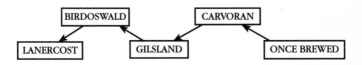

BIRDOSWALD   CARVORAN

LANERCOST   GILSLAND   ONCE BREWED

The next morning, after a hearty breakfast at Gibbs Farm, I was given a lift back to the Steel Rigg car park by Sarah Gibson, the daughter of Val who owns the farm. This is the fourth generation of Gibsons to farm here. Val's son runs the farm, which is committed to ethical policies, while Val runs the B&B and holiday cottage business, for they have diversified into the leisure industry by creating three self-catering cottages out of former outbuildings.

"Are you related to the Gibson who once owned Housesteads?" I had asked Val at breakfast time.

"No," she answered. "That was Hugh Gibson. He was one of the Hexham Gibsons. But my husband was a Scot and he always said he was a direct descendant of Bonnie Prince Charlie."

"How come?" I asked, truly astonished at this piece of information.

"We all used to laugh at his party piece," she answered, "until I did a bit of research and found that Charlie did in fact stay at Dumfries with the Gibsons who were farmers, and probably had his wicked way with the servant girl or suchlike."

See what I mean about the cross-fertilisation in Borderland?

Sarah Gibson who is a bundle of joy is in farming herself. She and her partner, she told me as we travelled, have a small two-acre organic farm not far away where they grow vegetables but she also teaches horticulture to young people with learning difficulties at an Agricultural College in Carlisle and had spent a year doing voluntary work in Botswana.

"We've just started beekeeping," she told me, in that lovely rolling Northumbrian accent. "We're making two sorts of honey. We've just started doing heather honey."

"How do you make that happen?" I asked in complete townie ignorance.

"You have to summer the bees so they get their nectar from the heather," she replied. "We'd been looking for somewhere to put the hives for a while and we knew there was lots of heather back of Skiddaw. So we drove round looking for somewhere and we found this old chap who'd got a property up there but he doesn't farm on it. We asked him if we could put our hives on his land and he agreed. We give him some of the honey."

"What about this organic farming? Why are you doing that? Isn't it more costly to do?" I asked.

"No, not really. But it's the way things are going, isn't it? Besides, it's better for the land not to keep on poisoning it," she said. "I want to take on some of the special needs people from college on to the farm, so we can do more. They're really patient and they work really hard. They're lovely people. There's our curlew."

She pointed into the valley.

"It's always there. I can tell the weather by it," Sarah told me. "Where did you stay before you came to us?"

"Green Carts," I said. "D'you know Sandra Maughan?"

"Aye," she smiled at me. "I was at school with her lads. This is it then."

She had pulled into the Steel Rigg car park to let me out. The lift, the openness of Sarah, the friendliness of Val, were all further examples of the warm welcome I was receiving here at Hadrian's northern frontier. This was not a land where people were closed in and brooding on their fate. Quite the opposite. Everyone I met was amazingly open. I felt constantly buoyed.

That morning's walk covers probably the most spectacular bit of the Hadrian's Wall Path, following the contours of the country as the Wall snakes up and down over greensward landscapes, across craggy outcrops and over steep indentations. Once again there was a light breeze in my face but the weather all day was warm and balmy and it was a pleasure to be out in it. Long sections of the Wall, some several courses high, accompany you on this stretch and you can see the bleakness of the countryside below you to the north with only the occasional farm breaking up the pastured scene. Over Windshields Crags the Hadrian's Wall Path is at its highest point and it is claimed that you can see four counties from up here – Northumberland, Durham, Cumbria and Dumfries and Galloway. I don't know if that's what I was seeing but you can certainly see for long distances south and north.

You'll notice plenty of evidence of the Roman settlement on this stretch because the landowners and the National Trust have maintained the Wall here and kept it in good condition. There are also the remains of milecastles and turrets, showing how Hadrian's basic plan for the Wall actually came into being. The general thinking is that the milecastles were small versions of the forts, designed to act as mechanisms for controlling the flow of traffic through the Wall, with gates to the north and the south. The turrets, on the other hand, are usually thought to have been watch-towers, guarded by a small number of squaddies, probably working on a rota.

If this is right, and the milecastles were official passing places, it's indicative of the Roman machine's adherence to a system which was against geographical reality and common sense. For, as you follow the line of the Wall, you come down from the heights to gaps between the hills. I've mentioned Busy Gap previously and that morning's walk took me through Peel Gap, Caw Gap and Hole Gap, through all of which there are now tracks or roads. These would have been the obvious places to site milecastles giving control of traffic, but then they wouldn't have been milecastles, would they? And Roman logic would have been challenged.

However, these gaps were the routes chosen at a different point of history.

Between the 13th and the 16th centuries, there was constant warfare and general lawlessness in this land that came to be known as the Borderlands. At the heart of this lawlessness were the Border Reivers, whose exploits make the American Wild West look like the Teddy Bears' Picnic. Robbery and blackmail (a word that comes from the Reivers' time) happened daily. Raiding, arson, kidnapping, murder and extortion were what many people in the Borderlands experienced as normality. At the centre of this territory was what was known as the Debatable Land, so called not because it housed a lot of peripatetic philosophers debating the meaning of life – I could have settled happily in that dispensation – but because ownership of it was constantly in dispute. Many of the most lawless families originated from the Debatable Lands.

For three centuries the names of Armstrong, Bell, Johnstone, Scott, Elliott, Nickson, Kerr, Dodd, Douglas, Regan and Graham feature prominently in the skirmishes reported. Three recent American presidents, viz. Johnson, Nixon and Reagan, owe their origins to the Border Reivers, not to mention the first man on the moon.

These Reivers were aware of the history around them and one of them had a bull called Caesar which he sold to his closest neighbour, who lived on the other side of the valley across a river.

"Men," Regan the Reiver said to his cowhands, "It's time to say our good-byes to this bull and take him across the river."

So the men roped Caesar and walked him down to the river.

They were about to put him on the boat to take him across, when Regan the Reiver's youngest son, who helped to raise Caesar, said with a tear in his eye, "Can we take him out for one last munch in his favourite meadow?"

The other hands agreed and led him just off the riverbank for a snack. Well, with the day as nice as it was, all of the hands took a quick nap. Four hours later, Regan the Reiver saw that the bull was still on his property and ran down into the valley.

He shouted and cursed at the men to wake them up. Once everyone was standing, he said that the beast should have been across the river long ago.

"In fact," he shouted angrily at them, "we've come to ferry Caesar, not to graze him!"

Hadrian was maybe the first to spot that this part of the land would produce problems unless properly fortified and protected, but subsequent kings of England and Scotland experienced similar problems. During this period the Borderlands were divided into six Marches, three on each side of the border, each of which was governed by a Warden. In reality these Wardens were just as crooked as the criminals they were appointed to capture and punish, for there are records of the Wardens involved in cattle-rustling and other larcenous activities. The local clans were the real rulers. To them cattle-rustling was second nature. They knew the lie of the land, including all the gaps between hills where they could easily ride through; they were skilled horsemen, whose small, light and unshod hobbler horses could negotiate the boggy mosslands well; and, through intermarriage and close alliances, they knew they could count on being rescued if they were arrested.

The most notorious of the Reivers was Kinmont Willie, one of the Armstrong clan, who used to ride with bands of up to 300 men, attacking several villages in one venture. One such sortie into Tynedale netted him and his men 1300 cattle, 60 horses and £2000 worth of goods, not to mention a good supply of Newcastle Brown Ale and several boxes of pork scratchings. In the course of it they burned down 60 houses and killed ten men. Kinmont Willie, however, was unceremoniously arrested on a Day of Truce when the local laws declared that the Wardens should meet to resolve differences and when all were supposedly immune from arrest. Willie, wanted for crimes against the English, was shackled and thrown into Carlisle gaol.

This so annoyed the Scots clans of the border – after all, there were laws regarding the Days of Truce, weren't there? Come on, chaps. Be fair! – that the Duke of Buccleugh with a gang of Armstrongs, Bells and Grahams broke into the prison and rescued the still-shackled Willie. They safely negotiated the flooded River Eden and rode home, stopping only to have Kinmont Willie's shackles chipped off by a blacksmith. He was soon back to his old tricks, raiding across the border, receiving stolen goods and organising illicit horse-trading for the rest of his life. The story of his arrest and rescue is told in one of those remarkable border poems, *The Ballad of Kinmont Willie*.

If you think Kinmont Willie is an odd name, try some of these out for size – Curst Eckie, Nebless Clem Croser, Archie Fire-the-Braes, Evilwillit Sandie, Hobbie Noble, As-it-Luiks, Hen-Harrow, Fingerless Will Nixon, Hob-the-King, Wynking Will, David-no-guide-Priest. Bob Bibby sounds almost normal by comparison.

It was through such passes as Peel Gap, Caw Gap and Hole Gap that the Reivers used to make their way. It is hard to imagine now, in this peaceful and wonderfully hospitable land, that in these border folk lie buried the genetic profiles of those murderous gangs, and yet the same family names persist on both sides of the border as a constant memorial to those bloodthirsty ways.

And so to Aesica, or Great Chesters, the next fort on the Wall, of which William Hutton reports:

> *"No buildings remain, except a modern farm-house, all the doors of which I found open, and none to guard the premises but a child, from whom I could gain no intelligence. There was no danger of a thief; for, in this solitary place, he must come a great way to take a little."*

The population of the farm that I passed was even smaller, for I saw no one, certainly not the Sixth Cohort of Nervians from Belgium, nor the Sixth Cohort of Raetians from Liechtenstein, nor the Second Cohort of Asturians from Spain, who were all stationed there at one time or other during the Roman occupation. Was the child whom Hutton met the descendant of one of these? This is not as daft as it might sound. Certainly there was found here a tombstone of a certain Aelius Mercurialis, who we know was of British descent and was recruited locally. It is thought he may have been the son of a retired auxiliary from one of the cohorts who had settled in the neighbourhood; Aelius Mercurialis may indeed have sowed his wild oats and been the child's antecedent.

Another remarkable feature here at Aesica is the remains of the aqueduct built by the Roman troops to bring a regular water supply to the fort from Fond Tom's Pool at the Head of the Caw Burn six miles away. You can see, if you look carefully to the north, how the line of the aqueduct ingeniously follows the contours of the hills in order to ensure a steady flow. Other than that, however, there's not much to see at Aesica. Excavations have taken place there sporadically, and during one of them in 1894 in the west gateway a hoard of jewelry was discovered. This comprised two brooches, three finger-rings, a necklace and a bracelet. The highlight was a beautiful gilt bronze brooch, with intricate Celtic designs, suggesting that the local population and those guarding the Wall had intermingled culturally as well as genetically.

After that, it's back on the grassy moorland as you follow long sections of the ditch over Cockmount Hill and then more ups and downs till you are descending from Walltown Crags to Walltown Quarry, which is now managed by the National Trust as a recreation area. As I passed along the lake I saw groups of schoolchildren, dressed in what looked like cardboard versions of Roman armour, being marched by some Roman centurion (or a teacher who wanted to look the part) around the opposite side. They were having a whale of a time, as was clear from the gurgling laughter that spread across the valley.

Just next to the Walltown Quarry is the Roman Army Museum at Carvoran, on the site of the fort known as Magna, at one time the home of the First Cohort of Syrian archers. Carvoran is administered by the Vindolanda Trust and shares the same desire to communicate with 21st-century folk about the Romans and to share the excitement that the Birleys and their fellows feel about the archaeological findings on Hadrian's Wall. I had great fun watching a recruiting film for the army and learning about the different weapons used by the squaddies. I was intrigued by the discovery from one of the Vindolanda tablets which told a lot about the basic diet of the soldiers. In one eight-day period squaddies were supplied with lard, pork fat, bacon lard, olive oil, ham, venison, pork, eggs, bread, beans, lentils, honey, semolina and, of course, several cans of Agri Cola. Not a bad diet, eh?

There was a description of the typical barracks block in a fort and I pictured in my mind those uncovered at Chesters and at Houseteads. Approximately 80 to 100 were housed in one such block, with eight bunk beds per room. The squaddies shared the cooking in each room, no doubt arguing as to whose turn it was to wash up, with the lucky ones getting an extra half an hour for a crafty fag, while the unlucky were forced to vent their frustration by scratching obscene graffiti on the walls.

Carvoran is another fine museum, with lots of interesting features, but I could not give it as much time as I might have done, for I still had lots to do on this my fourth day's walking. It is only a short distance from Carvoran to Gilsland, where I intended to pause for lunch but, shortly after leaving the Roman Army Museum, you come upon one of those ancient monuments that carries so much of the story of the Borderlands.

Thirlwall Castle is virtually on the line of Hadrian's Wall. It was built, using stones from the Wall inevitably, in the 14th century by the Thirlwall family as a fortified defence against the Scottish Reivers. After the union of Scotland and England in the early 18th century, the castle was abandoned and fell into ruin. It has recently been made safe and opened to the public, but there's not much to see. It's just another ruin, in truth, but its purpose was to keep those bloodthirsty Reivers out. If you listen carefully, you might hear on the wind *The Lament of the Border Widow*, whose reiver husband was hanged at his own door in 1529:

> *But think na ye my heart was sair*
> *When I laid the mould on his yellow hair?*
> *O think na ye my heart was wae*
> *When I turned about, away to gae?*
>
> *No living man I'll love again,*
> *Since that my lovely knight is slain,*
> *With ae lock of his yellow hair*
> *I'll chain my heart for evermair.*

On the other hand, you might not.

The approach to Gilsland features another section of the Wall and a well-defined part of the Vallum. As I entered Gilsland, I noticed a brightly-painted red shield and a sign outside a house proclaiming that here lives Jefficus, a former museum guide called Jeff Barnett who now operates as a one-man Roman soldier re-enactment show, visiting schools and some of the nearby Roman museums to demonstrate what it was like to be a squaddie in the legions.

I lunched on a sandwich and two pints of Greene King IPA beer at the Samson Inn in Gilsland. A notice-board gave the results of the local leek-growing competition alongside the pub team's position in the domino and cribbage leagues. Three big-built motorcyclists in full black leather outfits were drinking when I arrived and, after watching them knock back their pints, I was glad I was walking across country and not on the roads. Other Wall walkers joined me at the pub and we swapped a few boring anecdotes about our journey so far, which you'll be pleased to know I will not share with you.

Gilsland has an interesting history, much of it because of its associations with Sir Walter Scott, the Borders novelist. Scott visited Gilsland in 1797 while on a tour of the Lake District; here he met and fell hook, line and sinker for his future wife, Charlotte Carpenter. After a whirlwind romance, Scott proposed to Charlotte on a stone in the River Irthing, ever after known as the Popping Stone and the site of innumerable later marriage proposals, and five months later they were wed in Carlisle. Bless!

Scott subsequently used the Gilsland area as a setting for his novel *Guy Mannering* which features the unforgettable gipsy-woman, Meg Merrilees.

> *"She was full six feet high, wore a man's great-coat*
> *over the rest of her dress, had in her hand a goodly*

sloe-thorn cudgel, and in all points of equipment,
except her petticoats, seemed rather masculine than
feminine. Her dark elf-locks shot out like the snakes
of a gorgon, between an old-fashioned bonnet called
a bongrace, heightening the singular effect of her
strong and weather-beaten features, which they
partly shadowed, while her eye had a wild roll that
indicated something like real or affected insanity."

Meg Merrilees appears at a place called Mumps Ha' and it is believed that she was based on the real-life landlady of the Mumps Hall alehouse in Gilsland, Margaret Teasdale, a.k.a. Meg Mumps, who had a vile reputation for harbouring local villains and whose visiting travellers were rarely seen again. There was a story, used by Scott in *Guy Mannering*, of a certain Charlie Armstrong, of the noted Armstrong clan, who had sold his goods at Stagshaw Fair and stopped off for a pint at Mumps Hall on his way home, his pockets stuffed with money. Meg Mumps tried to entice him to stay the night but he refused and rode off. On the way he stopped to check his pistols and found they had been stuffed with tow, so he cleaned them out and reloaded them. When he was halted a short distance later by a bunch of bandits, he pulled his pistols out and shouted, "The tow's out!", whereupon the astonished gang rode off.

If only life were as simple as in Scott's romantic novels, the precursors to our own time's wonderful Mills & Boon tales. I have tried reading *Guy Mannering* recently but I'm sorry to say I was forced to give up by about page 30, when I found I couldn't engage with any of the characters and had no recall of any of the plot to that point. *Mea culpa*, I'm sure. So don't let me put you off. His books can be bought very cheaply from any second-hand book dealer.

Another former resting place in the village was Shaws Hotel which offered hot and cold baths and a sulphur bath, drawn from an underground well. In the 19th century this spa facility was very popular with the local gentry, who would visit to take the waters and seek relief from their stressful lives keeping the peasants from revolting. At the turn of the century, the premises were bought by Gilsland Spa Limited, which opened the building in 1901 as a convalescent home for members of the Co-operative Society in the north of England. This was a remarkably imaginative scheme for its time, and even more remarkable is the fact that it is still operating for the benefit of members of the Co-op. So you see, there is some point in collecting up the points for your divvy.

Just outside the village you come suddenly on the remains of the well-defined Milecastle 48 at Poltross Burn, in which you can see the beginnings of some steps inside the walls. Some argue that this proves that there must have been a rampart on top of the Wall for the soldiers to walk along, although a better explanation is that the steps merely led to the tower over the gateway. You also realise again how barmy some of this Roman insistence on order was, for the milecastle itself spreads over a very hilly field when surely common sense would have dictated a flatter surface would have been more sensible to build on. But no, everything had to be built by the rules and the rules said a milecastle every mile exactly. There will be no deviation. Still, I suppose the Roman Empire did last a few hundred years so they must have got something right.

Shortly after this milecastle you come upon another fine stretch of Hadrian's Wall leading down to the River Irthing, where once stood a massive Roman bridge. The river has changed course over the centuries but you can see the abutments where the Roman bridge would have begun. A modern footbridge takes you across the river and you then head uphill to another milecastle followed by a very long and impressive stretch of the Wall, which is ten courses high in many places. The original Wall westwards from the River Irthing was built of turf but it was rebuilt with stone at a later stage. There are many still-visible inscriptions at various points on this bit of Wall, most famously several phalluses. All the books tell you that this was not a piece of obscene graffiti but a symbol of luck and a charm against evil. The fact that one was found on the door of a brothel at Pompeii suggests to me that this is a bit of a cover-up. Soldiers, after all, were hot-blooded males; it would not be surprising to find that their twin instincts were fighting and sex, would it?

Birdoswald, or Banna, is the fort that you reach at the end of this stretch of graffiti'd Wall. It is different from the earlier Roman forts visited because the site was built over a number of times. The oldest records tell of property being there from 1200 but it is from the time of the Border Reivers that the current building owes its origins. The farm buildings were not strong enough to resist the raiders, so a bastle house was added some time in the 15th or 17th century. The main part of the current farmhouse was built in 1745 by Anthony Bowman, whose son was visited in 1801 by William Hutton, who reports the visit thus:

> *"When I entered the house of Mr Bowman, who is the proprietor, and occupier, of these once imperial premises, I was received with that coldness which indicates an unwelcome guest, bordering upon a dismission; for an ink-bottle and book are suspicious emblems. But, as information was the grand point in view, I could not, for trifles, give up my design; an expert angler will play with his fish till he can catch him.*

> *"With patience, with my small stock of rhetoric, and, above all, the simplicity of my pursuit, which was a powerful argument, we became exceedingly friendly; so that the family were not only willing to let me go, but obliged me to promise a visit on my return. They gave me their best; they wished it better. I had been, it seems, taken for a person employed by Government to examine private property, for the advancement of taxation."*

No such problems affected my visit. Birdoswald is now managed by English Heritage and the staff could not have been more helpful, even with my small rhetoric. I purchased a copy of the guidebook and asked if it could be posted to my home to save adding weight to my bag. This was arranged with exemplary courtesy, so much so that I indulged in a slice of cherry cake and a cup of tea in the neat tea-rooms beyond the counter, before beginning my exploration.

You may be tired, like I was by now, of hearing about the playing-card shape of the fort, the altars, the granaries, the *principia*, the gatehouses and all that sort of standard Roman fort stuff. I must admit there were times when I wished there had been a bit more variation in the designs – maybe the odd potting shed here and there, or a garage for the commandant's chariot. But there is something at Birdoswald which is not found in other forts and that is the remains of the *basilica exercitatoria* (drill and exercise hall), only discovered in 1989. It is a huge space, roughly 140 feet by 52 feet, and half of it is still stuck underneath the farmhouse, but it was used undoubtedly for the squaddies to exercise in during the frequent bad weather that visitors to the north still expect to experience for most of the year.

There's not another drill hall like this found in any fort throughout the Roman Empire, so it's a bit special, even though, when you stand there gazing at the site with its pitifully few remnants, it is difficult to believe that. You need to make a leap of imagination, maybe using the excellent drawing in the guidebook, to get a sense of how this building might have been used. In the *basilica exercitatoria* the squaddies would have first undertaken gymnastic exercises, probably not dramatically different from the sorts of touch-your-toes, stretch-your-arms, run-on-the-spot type of thing that I suffered in P.E. at school. As far as we know, the Romans were the first to ensure systematic training for their professional army. They knew that the legionary and the auxiliary had to be, first and foremost, physically stronger than his enemy. Roman writers tell us that the soldiers would have also done their weapons training with wooden swords and reed shields, as well as the inevitable marching drills (*sinister, dexter* (left, right); *sinister, dexter; sinister, dexter*). Hadrian himself is known to have decreed a set of training measures to the army which were still in use 200 years after his death.

Stand and gaze at this *basilica exercitatoria* and think of those poor squaddies, going through the motions of training exercises, some no doubt keen to toughen themselves up but most, I suspect, just thinking about getting down to the pub for a few beers later on in the evening.

"Not another bloody milecastle!"

I was beginning to sympathise with my walking companion, a young New Zealand woman whom I'd joined up with on leaving Birdoswald for the late afternoon walk that was to take me to my night's resting place.

Kiri, whose legs were heavily strapped, told me she had damaged both her ankles while walking the Kerry Way in Ireland, having damaged her knee skiing in Canada a year earlier, and that this was her first journey since surgery. She was following the Hadrian's Wall path in preparation for planned walks along the Pembrokeshire Coastal Path, which she hoped to complete in ten days, and then along the Southern Coastal Path, which would take her a further two and a half months. Then she was going home. She was indubitably mad.

"I love the wind in my face, and the hospitality up here has been something else," she said, adjusting her heavy pack on her shoulders. "But I've seen enough turrets, milecastles and forts to last a bloody lifetime!"

The Wall virtually disappears around here. There are only a

few traces of it visible after Birdoswald. We passed the Pike Hill signal tower, a remnant which proves that the Romans used some kind of semaphore system to communicate between sections of the Wall, and then Hare Hill, which was once erroneously thought to be the highest point on the Wall. Here a stone was discovered bearing the inscription "PP", which would have been the mark of the *primus pilus* or the chief centurion. What would his day have been like? Here's an extract from the diary of one such:

6.00 Trumpet call. Got up, shouted at soldiers.
7.00 Breakfast – Scott's porridge oats again. Can't wait for the next supply of Cumberland sausage.
8.00 Took parade. Bollocked a few soldiers, just for the hell of it. Sent the cohort on route march.
9.00 Back to bed with *The Sun*. Looks like problems in Germany again. Bloody Krauts!

I was reaching the end of my fourth day, as you can perhaps tell. Two more days and I would have completed my trek. I said goodbye to Kiri and took a track downhill and south towards Lanercost and the Abbey Bridge Inn.

That evening, after a hearty meal of steak pie and vegetables followed by a home-made apple and blackcurrant pie, washed down by three tasty pints of Coniston Bluebird beer, I sat outside in the warmth of the late evening sun on the old bridge across the River Irthing, talking to Sue Hatt, who with her husband owns the Abbey Bridge Inn.

"How long have you been here?" I asked, aware that there had must have been substantial refurbishment in recent times.

"We bought it four years ago," Sue, a tall blonde woman with darting eyes, told me. "It had been closed for two years when we bought it. We've spent a lot on it. I was running a school in the dales at the same time and my husband has a full-time job, so it's been tough. But we did it."

"Did you have a job getting the locals back?" I queried, sipping my pint.

"At first, yes," she told me. "But gradually we've won them round. Most of our trade is residential. We get lots of walkers from Hadrian's Wall, like yourself. And lots of them come back with their husbands and wives."

I made a mental note to do the same. The Abbey Bridge is situated in a lovely, serene setting, just the other side of the 1732 bridge over the river, whose gurgling waters sent me to sleep contented that night.

X

HADRIAN THE SQUADDIE

Ever since homo became sapiens, he demonstrated that he could also be a bit of a sap. Why? Because, whenever he got a bit upset about another male of the species treading on his cabbages or eyeing up his woman, his first reaction was to start bashing the other one up. Now such behaviour is not unusual in the animal kingdom, where defending your territory and seeking exclusive breeding rights with the female of the species are pretty normal reasons for baring the fangs or flapping the wings or whatever form of aggressive behaviour seems best suited.

What makes humans different is the capacity to form into bands in order to duff up other bands of humans. We call this war and some experts think that it was technology that led to war. First of all humans hunted other species with their bare hands, then, as they discovered they could use sharp-edged stones to kill animals, it sort of made sense to join together in this exercise and to share the spoils. It wasn't long, of course – a few thousand years perhaps – before they started to use these flinty knives and, later, clubs, spears and arrows to chase off the visiting neighbours who, whatever the appearance to the contrary, had really only popped round for a chat and a cup of warming lamb's urine. This was such good fun, if you won, that pretty soon it became the only game in town and in most societies across the world.

And, of course, when this is the best game around, it's not too difficult to discover other reasons for going to war. Pinching someone else's woman was – surprise, surprise – a very strong runner-up to territorial invasion in the excuses for a punch up. And if it was an alpha-plus woman, even better. Witness Helen of Troy.

So a warrior class developed in many prehistoric societies and those warriors became the forerunners of armies, some of the earliest of which are found in Egypt. There, in the fertile lands that developed around the Nile Delta, people settled and prospered and, as their living conditions steadily improved, their life expectancy increased and bingo! you get the start of a population explosion. The solution? Easy, extend your boundaries and pinch some territory from your neighbours. Result? The neighbours, unsurprisingly, say "No go, Pharaoh" and pretty soon it's war and armies and bloodshed and all the rest of it.

The Roman army was perhaps the inevitable end-result of all those thousands of years of pre-history. Initially formed by the farmer-settlers of early Rome to fight off the invading Gauls from France, who carried strings of onions, smoked Gauloises and quoted Jean-Paul Sartre, and then later the invading Carthaginians from North Africa, led by Hannibal and his circus elephants, the Roman army became the finest fighting force of ancient times. As I've shown earlier, it was so good that, in the end, it became the reason for the Roman Empire and, until the time of Hadrian, it was unable to give up conquering other lands and expanding its grasp over the world.

As in so much else that Rome did, the Roman army pinched all the best ideas from elsewhere, chucked them into the melting pot, and came up with something entirely novel and excruciatingly effective. So, it adopted the phalanx formation that the Greeks had invented, whereby a squad of soldiers fought in close formation using their shields to protect them as they engaged in hand-to-hand combat with their spears. The Romans developed this into the more flexible *maniple*. This consisted of about 180 men, with each man given about five square yards fighting and manoeuvring room. Each maniple was separated from the next by about 20 yards and the formation was staggered, like a chess board, so that, if the leading *maniple* were repulsed or fancied nipping off for a quiet moment, the following one could easily take its place in the battle. The Romans also used the new technology of the sword rather than the somewhat unwieldy spear. The result was that the Roman legion was not surpassed by another army in its tactical ability and its killing capacity for almost 1,500 years.

Now add to the equation the Romans' ability to support their troops logistically by means of the extensive road network that they built. It is reckoned that some 240,000 miles of military roads were built during the heyday of the Roman Empire and, where these roads were paved, as in the major land routes, the legions could march 20 miles a day along them, with all their equipment and baggage. Next add the development of specialised tactics, such as the *testudo* or tortoise, whereby the *maniple* of soldiers could advance with their shields positioned above their heads and to their fronts, rears and sides in order to provide maximum protection, or the *onager*, a high-powered form of catapult that could hurl a 100 pound stone 400 yards.

And, finally, remember that the Roman army was made up not of farmers clubbing together to defend their properties, nor of conscripts who'd rather be out skateboarding or charioteering but had been ordered by the state to do their duty on behalf of their fellow-citizens, nor of johnny-come-lately mercenaries hired to fight the battles of others. No, the Roman army was a regular army, with wages for its troops, permanent barracks and arsenals, centralised manufacture of swords and shields and uniforms, and an organisational pattern and methodology that was the envy of the ancient world.

What was it really like being in the Roman army?

The Roman Army museum at Carvoran does a pretty fine job in giving you a picture of military life at the Empire's furthest reaches. I really enjoyed the army recruiting film on regular show in one room. In this film members of the Ermine Street Guard re-enactment group kit themselves out in some pseudo-Roman outfits and act out some choice moments from the imagined life of a Roman squaddie to show what recruits might be in for. It's clever educational stuff, though it doesn't quite match up to the sort of high-tech, whizz-bang advertising that the armed forces nowadays use to attract wannabe heroes into their ranks. There's no high-powered chariots on offer; there's no promises of trips to exotic locations (though, thinking about it, I suppose Hadrian's Wall was the exotic location); and there's no reference to the hordes of screaming local wenches that would fall at your feet just gagging for it. But the basic attraction is the same really – "Easy life! Lots of Respect! Very little danger! See the world! Good Pay!" – or words to that effect, though it's done in Latin, of course.

What you do find out from the film, however, is some of the basic stuff, such as that only Roman citizens could be in the legions. Everyone else had to join the auxiliaries and there were just as many of them as there were in the legions and their organisation paralleled that of the legions, because this was the Romans' smart scheme for preventing the young bucks of countries they conquered from fomenting trouble back at home.

Now what always puzzled me was that there could never have been enough people living in Rome itself to make up the full complement of the legions in the army and I somehow doubt if there were sufficient in the whole of Italy to maintain a permanent army of the size we're talking about. But then I realised that many of the lands conquered early on by the Romans, particularly Spain and France, became extensions of the state and their peoples were awarded citizen status. Add to that the descendants of retired auxiliaries, who were also awarded citizen status after their 25 year service, and the numbers start to add up.

Just imagine for a moment or two that you have been successful in your quest to join a legion in the Roman army. You've proved your citizenship because your papers (that you bought for a few quid on the black market from a scurvy slave, who once worked for Hadrian's auntie's second cousin's cook) show that you really are descended from Romulus and Remus. You've reached your 18th birthday and are prepared to sign on for the next 25 years. You've shown that you're a bit of a muscleman, so all those days in the gym pumping iron have done the business. And you've shown that you can read, write and calculate. Not many people realise this but you had to be pretty literate and numerate to manage in the Roman army. There were all those instruction manuals to start off with – how to pitch a tent in a force ten gale, how to get your shield into the right position in the testudo formation, how to fire an onager, or how to avoid catching venereal diseases from the local girls. The ability to do sums was necessary so you could calculate how much of your pay was still owing to you, work out the number of marching steps you would need to take to reach the next milepost, and, crucially, in the engineering works carried out by the soldiers in the construction of roads, aqueducts, bridges, camps and forts. Not forgetting, of course, the Wall.

Once you're accepted and you've been allocated to one of the legions, it's time for your training. The first thing you'll be taught is how to march. *"Sinister, dexter; sinister, dexter; sinister, dexter."* That would be the command that came bellowing out of the centurion's mouth as he taught you the necessity of marching in time and in line, because the Romans recognised that an army which could be split up because some of the soldiers at the rear were struggling to keep up was an army that could be attacked. But, as well as learning to march in line, you had to learn to march quickly. Regular route marches were undertaken to ensure you could walk 20 miles in five hours carrying a pack that weighed 60 to 70 pounds. These would take place throughout your career, not just in your basic training, so the troops on Hadrian's Wall would have had to do their fair share of route marches, just to ensure their continued fitness and show that they could still hack it.

Then there was weapons training, using pretend weapons – wickerwork shields, wooden swords and wooden javelins, a bit like in *Dad's Army*, except that these pretend jobs were twice the weight of the real thing. The idea was that, if you could manage with these ultra-heavyweight weapons, you'd be fine when you got on to the battlefield with the real McCoy. With these dummy weapons, you'd be pitched against six-foot high wooden poles, until you became sharp enough to practice with a fellow-recruit. More advanced weapons training used some of the methods employed in the teaching of gladiators, so, if you really wanted to end up looking like Russell Crowe, you'd have to submit yourself to this, still using heavy wooden swords and shields to weigh you down. If you were useless at weapons training, you had your rations cut and were given barley instead of wheat.

Although a drill and exercise hall was sometimes built inside the fort, as seen at Birdoswald, on Hardknott Pass, where a Roman army garrison protected the route from Ambleside in the central Lake District to Ravenglass fort on the west coast, there is a parade ground where similar exercises would have taken place in the open air. Given the winter winds up on the tops in the north of England, I know which fort I'd have rather served in. Though, to tell the truth, my military career would never have amounted to much in the first place. Given my luck, I'd have probably ended up as the official letter-writer to the troops.

The soldiers who were stationed on the Wall once it had been built were auxiliaries from all over the Empire. Their job, as far as can be understood, was to patrol the Wall and keep a look out for any crafty Caledonians trying to nip through with illegal loads of woad. We don't know what the military routines would have been like for these soldiers but, given that there were milecastles, and two turrets between each milecastle, and forts with gateways, there was clearly no shortage of places that needed regular patrolling. Then there would have been the scouting parties sent out into the land of the Jocks to see if any of them were fomenting any trouble, plus the maintenance of the forts themselves and of the Wall, the ditch and the Vallum.

And, of course, there were any number of jobs that needed doing within the forts, for an army is a society in minuscule and needs all the services that a smallish village would need. One list of soldiers not required to perform military duties includes the following: ditch diggers, farriers, master builders, pilots, shipwrights, ballista makers, glaziers, smiths, arrow makers, coppersmiths, helmet makers, wagon makers, roof-tile makers, sword cutlers, water engineers, trumpet makers, horn makers, bow makers, plumbers, blacksmiths, masons, lime burners, woodcutters, charcoal burners, butchers, huntsmen, keepers of sacrificial animals, grooms and tanners.

You do wonder what the pilots were doing in the Roman army, don't you? Had the Romans secretly mastered the art of flying? Or were they training up human cannonballs to be fired from the *onager*?

The guys who were responsible for organising the training of the troops and generally for keeping them in tip-top condition were the centurions, each of whom was responsible for 80 squaddies. These were the senior NCOs of the Roman army – the equivalent of Sergeant-Majors really – and the chief centurion was known as *primus pilus*, literally the Number One Javelin. Centurions could rise through the ranks but the officer class came from the Roman aristos. Top of the pile was the legate, the chief commander of the legion, and assisting him was a tribune. Both came from the upper echelons of Roman society and it was generally the way to political success later in life to have achieved something or other in the military.

Hadrian, like most young aristocrats, did his time in the army. He enrolled as a 14-year-old in the military training school in his home town of Italica. At the age of 19 he was sent as the military tribune to the II Adiutrix Legion in modern Hungary. This was almost certainly an important education for the future Emperor, because the II Adiutrix had spent 15 years campaigning in Britain, some of which was under Agricola. Many of the soldiers would have had tales to tell of the Battle of Mons Graupius and of the strange Caledonians with their woad-painted bodies, shouting "Hoots, mon". A year later, in A.D. 96, he was transferred to a similar post in what is now Macedonia; and a year after that he was doing the same job in northern Germany. Here he would have seen for himself the new system of forts and watchtowers that were being built to enable the Roman troops to keep a watchful eye on the barbarians to the north and east.

In that same year of A.D. 98 Trajan became Emperor and Hadrian returned to Rome with him, and began his political career, but in A.D. 106 he was back with the squaddies again, this time as boss, i.e. legate, of the I Minervia Legion in Lower Germany. Here he was serving Trajan again in one of the latter's endless wars and is said to have achieved great things, though we don't know what they were and those who wrote this were probably just buttering up the Emperor in the way that smarmy folk at court always have done. At the end of that particular war, Hadrian was sent to act as legate in charge of his old legion, II Adiutrix, with whom he had served his first post. By A.D. 108 he was back in Rome, having experienced a fair amount of life in the military. He had seen battle, he had witnessed how the army kept tabs on the barbarians, he had seen the putative barriers of Germany, and he would no doubt have heard tales about the land of the Brits and what went on there.

But what else did he do, apart from what was required of him for his military duties? Indeed, what else did any of the squaddies do when they were not on duty?

I guess that off-duty life in a Roman fort was pretty much like off-duty life in any army. There would have been some polishing of the sword and armour with Brasso, some washing of the tunics and sewing up the holes in the same, and some relaxation in the bath house. There would inevitably have been some game-playing and you can see evidence of this in the counters and boards found on display in Segedunum and Vindolanda. These board games included, appropriately enough, The Little Soldiers, which was rather like draughts, and the Game of Twelve Lines, a forerunner of backgammon. The loaded dice at Vindolanda show that there were cheats in the Roman army as well as in modern ones.

Hadrian was known for being quite a skilled player of the *cithara*, an ancestor of the guitar. No doubt squaddies in the forts on the Wall, like soldiers everywhere, would have enjoyed a bit of late night singing after an evening of bending the arm with some select Lambrusco, recently delivered from the wine merchant in York, or even some Belgian beer, concocted on site by the local brewer. Maybe the troops on the Wall would have enjoyed singing the following song, accompanied by Hadrian on his *cithara*, entitled *Woad Ode*, to the tune of *Men of Harlech*:

> *What's the use of wearing braces ?*
> *Vests and pants and boots with laces ?*
> *Spats and hats you buy in places*
> *Down the Brompton Road ?*
> *What's the use of shirts of cotton ?*
> *Studs that always get forgotten ?*
> *These affairs are simply rotten,*
> *Better far is woad.*
> *Woad's the stuff to show men.*
> *Woad to scare your foemen.*
> *Boil it to a brilliant hue*
> *And rub it on your back and your abdomen.*
> *Ancient Briton ne'er did hit on*
> *Anything as good as woad to fit on*
> *Neck or knees or where you sit on.*
> *Tailors you be blowed!!*

Romans came across the channel
All dressed up in tin and flannel.
Half a pint of woad per man'll
Dress us more than these.
Saxons you can waste your stitches
Building beds for bugs in britches.
We have woad to clothe us which is
Not a nest for fleas.
Romans keep your armours.
Saxons your pyjamas.
Hairy coats were made for goats,
Gorillas, yaks, retriever dogs and llamas.
Tramp up Snowdon with your woad on,
Never mind if you get rained or blowed on.
Never want a button sewed on.
Go it Ancient B's!!

No doubt the squaddies also cursed the northern weather, the Picts, the midges, the centurions, the officers, the food they were served, the tasks they were given, and each other. They would have called each other *mentula* (dickhead), *pedicator* (bugger), *pathicus* (sodomite), *irrumator* (bastard) and so on. They would have boasted about their Friday night conquests at the local taverns where they'd picked up prostitutes and they'd have looked forward to the next Friday night or the next leave when they'd get extended opportunities for sex. For these were young, virile, healthy men in their full sexual prime, stuck at the end of the Empire away from the women of their own homelands. Is it any wonder that sexual matters would have been foremost in their minds?

Finally, in these days before TV, before radio, before novels, before printing even, the squaddies would have amused each other by telling stories so, to finish this look at the life of a soldier on the Wall, here's a typical story that might have been told in those days.

Julius Caesar was addressing the crowd on the Capitol.

"Friends, Romans and Countrymen, lend me your ears. Tomorrow I take our glorious army to conquer Northern Europe and I shall start with France. We shall kill many Gauls and return victorious."

The crowd are up on their feet. "Yeeeeeeeeeeeeeeeeeeeeees, hail mighty Caesar."

Brutus turns to his mate and says, "He doesn't half talk some rubbish eh? He couldn't fight his way out of a wet parchment bag."

Six months later, Caesar comes back having conquered France and addresses the crowd on the Capitol.

"Friends, Romans and Countrymen, I have returned from our campaign in France and as I promised, we killed 50,000 Gauls."

The crowd are up on their feet again. "Yeeeeeeeeeeeeeeeeeeeeees, hail mighty Caesar."

Brutus once again turns to his mate and says, "I'm sick of his nonsense, I'm off to France to check this out."

So Brutus sets off for France and three weeks later he comes back to Rome. Caesar is addressing the public on the Capitol again.

"Friends, Romans and Countrymen, tomorrow we set off for Britain and we are going to sort those bastards out."

The crowd are up on their feet. "Yeeeeeeeeeeeeeeeeeeeeeeeeeeeees, hail mighty Caesar."

Brutus jumps up and shouts, "Caesar, you are a liar. You told us that you had killed 50,000 Gauls in France but I've been there to check it out and you only killed 25,000."

The crowd are stunned and all sit down in silence.

Caesar gets up and looks slowly round the Capitol then across at Brutus and says, "Brutus, you are forgetting one thing......... Away Gauls count double in Europe."

XI

CROSS-COUNTRY TO CARLISLE

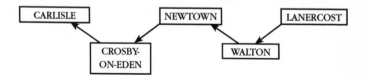

Lanercost Priory is really nothing much to look at, to be honest, though the adjoining church is rather splendid. Following the dissolution of the monasteries in 1536 much of it fell into rack and ruin, though part of it was restored 200 years later and used as the parish church, which it still is, and a delightful one at that. But don't be put off by all that, for its blackened old walls hold a fascinating story – the story of Edward Longshanks, the Hammer of the Scots, as he liked to think of himself.

Edward I was a bit like the Romans, in fact. He was intent on expanding by force his control of Britain and successfully overcame the forces of the Welsh prince Llewellyn ap Gruffud, before turning his attention to the Jocks. Lanercost Priory and its peace-loving monks were frequently disturbed by Longshanks's presence, for he used Lanercost as his base for forays into Scotland on a number of occasions. The Jocks were led at this time, of course, by the famous Robert the Bruce and his spider, with whom Edward got caught up in the webs of many a battle. Two of Bruce's brothers were hung, drawn and quartered on Longshanks's orders, and their decapitated heads were brought to him at Lanercost, so he could bounce ping-pong balls off them after dinner.

In 1306, on one of his forays to the north, intent on harrying the aforesaid Robert the Bruce (and his spider), Edward was taken ill at Lanercost. Now having royalty come to stay with you might look like a smart kind of thing to do but, believe me, it was, and certainly still is, a costly business. As well as Edward, there were seven valets, 23 pack-horse drivers responsible for the royal household's goods, 45 drivers and 22 grooms for the general baggage, two servants responsible for the books and ornaments of the chapel, 59 servants responsible for work in the kitchen, buttery, almonry, wardrobe and other departments, plus the various other toadies of the royal court. 200 people had to be accommodated altogether. They were not what you might call welcome visitors, as Steeleye Span's song *Lanercost* suggests:

> *The priests go down to the river to fish for Friday's meal*
> *The King is brooding day and night*
> *Black with hate, cursing fate*
> *To be ill when the foe is in sight.*

Edward's illness worsened and his stay at Lanercost went on and on. The monks thought they'd never see the back of him and his entourage. Doctors tried all sorts on the king – oil of teberinth, fragrant powders, enemas, syrups, purgative drugs, balsam, beta-blockers, and various herbal cures. But none worked, so, just in case, they laid in a stock of embalming spices as well. Finally, after the best part of six months, Edward and his court, plus their embalming spices, left for Carlisle and a further destination which you will discover more about later.

After Edward left, the monks were so brassed off with what had happened that they decided to take a vow of silence. They rarely spoke. Each day began with morning worship. The service started when the head abbot came in and chanted,

"Good morning."

"Good morning," the monks chanted in reply.

They said not another word until evening vespers, when the

head abbot came in and chanted,

"Good evening."

The monks all replied in unison, "Good evening."

Not another word was spoken until the next morning.

Several months later one of the monks decided he had to break up the boredom of this routine. The next morning the head abbot chanted,

"Good morning."

"Good morning," all the other monks responded,

But the one bored monk, hiding his identity from the other monks, chanted,

"Good evening."

Quickly, the head abbot sang in reply,

"Someone chanted evening. He must be a stranger."

There's a fine display in the church, telling the story of Edward Longshanks's stay at Lanercost and of the subsequent history of the Priory. The royal hangers-on with their embalming fluids were not the only ones who didn't expect Edward to live much longer. He himself gave instructions to his son, soon to be Edward II, that on his death, his body was to be boiled and the bones were to be placed in a chest and carried at every battle, while the heart was to be encased in a casket and taken to the Holy Land and buried there. When death did come, Edward II, more intent on getting his lover Piers Gaveston back from exile in France, ignored his father's orders.

The Lanercost monks may have been pleased to see the back of the king but Robert the Bruce did not forget the priory's part in the cruelty inflicted on prisoners and their hospitality, reluctantly given as it might have been, to the royal entourage. After Edward I's death and while Edward II was still dallying with his lover, Robert descended on Lanercost, threw all the monks in prison and grabbed what remaining wealth they had. His grandson carried on the good work two generations later by setting fire to the buildings. Lovely people, weren't they?

That Wednesday morning I left Lanercost to rejoin the Wall walk near what the Ordnance Survey map tells me is Milecastle 54 but which is actually invisible. The countryside is much more gentle, away from the dramatic heights of the Whin Sill. This is mostly arable land with cows and sheep grazing peacefully wherever you look. The course of the Wall is barely visible now, though occasional stones pushing through the grass remind you that you are still on its line and the Vallum is clearly evident to the south.

After passing the Centurion pub in Walton, with its banner proudly proclaiming it has been named 'Countryside Pub of the Year', the path takes you on the line of the ditch through a small copse. At the end of this, some enterprising vicar has placed a milk churn with "Please open" written on it. You can't fail to be tempted, can you? So I opened it and found a request for a donation towards the repair costs of the church in Walton. Full marks for imagination, 50p for the church funds.

Just south of here, curiously situated between the Vallum and the Wall itself was another Roman fort, known as Camboglanna. William Hutton reports on its status in 1801 thus:

> *"The works are wholly gone; for a gentleman, who, like other 'wise men from the east', had acquired a fortune in India, recently purchased the estate*

*on which this Castle stood, for thirteen thousand
pounds, stocked up the foundation, and erected
a noble house on the spot. Other Stations preserve
the ruins, but this only in name; and this is the first
which has been sacrificed to modern taste."*

The gentleman, whose descendants still own Castlesteads, was
called John Johnson and he did a very good job, as Hutton says, in
destroying the Roman fort's remains. There have been occasional
excavations over the years which have unearthed evidence that
the fort was garrisoned at various times by troops of Dacians
from modern-day Romania, Gauls from France, Batavians from
Germany, and Tungrians from Belgium. It's of interest, given this
mutli-cultural presence, that an inscription from a temple just
outside the fort walls was dedicated to "The Mother goddesses of
all nations". But there's nothing now to show of this fort and its
multi-racial inhabitants, thanks to the depredations of that "wise
man from the east".

Newtown, a mile or so further on, is exactly what its name
suggests, though town is maybe a bit strong. It's really a posh
dormitory village for Carlisle, where all the old cottages have
been tarted up and even the old church and school have been
converted into bijou dwellings. The path now marches along
through the old ditch, for there are no visible signs of the Wall
itself hereabouts, though it is commemorated in the name of
another tiny settlement, Oldwall. Just past here at a path junction
a sign invites the casual walker to detour to the Sportsman pub in
nearby Laversdale, offering a lift back to the Path after imbibing.
More Borderlands generosity, though I did not this time indulge
in it.

The skies were buzzing just south of here, because the former
R.A.F. Crosby airbase has become Carlisle Airport, on whose
grounds stands the Edward Haughey Solway Aviation Museum,
which is well worth a few quid of anybody's money to visit. The
museum houses an impressive display showing the development

of powered flight "from simple air-cooled radial engines to the complexity of the modern turbofan by way of the famous Rolls Royce Merlin". Real anorak stuff, in other words. But, and it is a big but, the museum also tells the fascinating story of the Blue Streak rocket, which was the UK's 1950s attempt at matching the USSR and USA in developing an Intermediate Range Ballistic Missile. In other words, Blue Streak was intended to provide the means whereby we could bomb the hell out of the Russkis with nuclear weapons. This, at the time I was growing up, was part of what was called the nuclear deterrent. Just imagine if the Picts had decided to ape the Roman *testudo*, to make their own *onagers*, to use the same weapons. That would have resulted in the same sort of stalemate as the Cold War and Hadrian would have had no need to build his Wall.

Carlisle airport is actually owned by Edward Haughey, the multimillionaire owner of Norbrook Pharmaceuticals, which produces veterinary pharmaceuticals; he is also a Senator in the upper house of the Eire parliament and has recently been given a seat in the House of Lords. The son of a cattle-dealer, he has come a long way and is not afraid to show off his wealth. He owns large estates in Ireland and in Cumbria and has a castle in the middle of each.

I watched the planes landing and taking off from Carlisle Airport as I marched along the Hadrian's Wall Path, finally leaving the line of the invisible Wall and turning south towards Crosby-on-Eden where I stopped for lunch. The Stag at Crosby is beside the main road on the line of the Stanegate, and here I enjoyed a pleasant couple of pints of Jennings's Cumberland Ale and an appropriate Roma baguette, which turned out to be stuffed with chicken, tomato, mozarella and cucumber and was very tasty.

Jennings's Brewery is the sponsor of the Hadrian's Wall Path Passport scheme. Jennings is a Cumbrian brewer, based in Cockermouth, and I guess the decision to sponsor the Passport scheme made good advertising sense. In fact, the Stag at Crosby is the only brewery-owned pub on the Hadrian's Wall Path but, as you will have noticed, its beers are available in many of the other pubs along the way. The most commonly found beer is the Cumberland Ale but, if you search hard, you can find some of their other exquisite creations – Crag Rat, Cocker Hoop, Old Smoothy, Cross Buttock (named after a Cumberland wrestling throw), La'al Cockle Warmer, and Sneck Lifter. It's almost worth walking the Wall to get a taste of Jennings's. Definitely not to be missed.

The afternoon's walk was an uneventful stroll along the banks of the River Eden into Carlisle itself, passing Linstock Castle, originally the home of the Bishops of Carlisle, later used as a pele tower to protect against the Border Reivers, but now a farmhouse, and then into the grounds of Rickerby Park. The Head family once lived here, one of whom was the oddly-named George Head Head who was responsible for the curious shapes on the buildings you pass as you enter the park. Another scion of the same family, Joseph Monkhouse Head, was a renowned Carlisle banker in the early 19th century who is commemorated in an unusual fashion at Eden School. Head forgot the keys to his bank one day and was aware that, to avoid a run on the bank by investors, he had to open by 10.00 am. So he sent his nephew scuttling back to Rickerby House to fetch the keys, and he managed to return in the nick of time, thus saving the bank and Joseph Head's fortune. The Key Race is still performed every year at Eden School in memory of this event. Fascinating stuff, eh?

The brown sandstone Carlisle Castle stands on an imposing site at the northern edge of the city. Its keep dates back to the 12th century when Henry I decided to fortify this most northerly outpost of England, but recent excavations have shown that there were three Roman forts on the same site at different times. Carlisle Castle has witnessed plenty of history in its time. One of its governors was Henry IV's brother-in-law Ralph Neville, who as Earl of Westmorland appears in Shakespeare's Henry IV (Parts 1 & 2) and Henry V. Remember this?

We few, we happy few, we band of brothers;
For he today that sheds his blood with me
Shall be my brother; be he ne'er so vile,
This day shall gentle his condition:
And gentlemen in England now a-bed
Shall think themselves accurs'd they were not here
And hold their manhoods cheap while any speaks
That fought with us upon Saint Crispin's day.

Yes, that was bold Henry addressing the Earl of Westmorland, the same Ralph Neville, before the battle of Agincourt. Another governor was Elizabeth I's champion George Clifford, and Richard, Duke of Gloucester, later to become Dick Deterred, a.k.a. Richard III, also ruled the northern lands from here. In fact, Shakespeare seems to have drawn on Carlisle Castle for more than one of his characters, for his Macbeth has links here as well.

You wouldn't Adam and Eve it but Shakespeare actually got the story of Macbeth wrong. It turns out that Duncan was not a nice old king at all but a bit of a bastard. Macbeth, on the contrary, who admittedly did kill Duncan, was a pretty damn fine ruler for nigh on seventeen years. Lady Macbeth, whose real name was Gruach, was a bit of a sweetie, and neither Banquo, nor Macduff nor the witches existed. The one part that Shakespeare got right was the bit about Duncan's son Malcolm invading Scotland and killing Macbeth. And what's it all got to do with Carlisle? Well, you see Malcolm was the Earl of Cumberland and his base was Carlisle. But really, Will, you should have checked your sources a bit better. If the truth got out, who knows what might happen?

Inevitably, given its position at the frontier, most of the castle's action has involved the centuries-old warfare between the English and the Scots and in fact it was occupied by Scottish kings on more than one occasion. However, there are three particular moments in that long history which are of special interest.

I've told you about the warfare between Edward Longshanks

and Robert the Bruce and how that impacted on Lanercost Priory, but Carlisle Castle saw its bit of the action too. Longshanks was not going to be called the Hammer of the Scots for nothing, so he made Carlisle the base for his assault on south-west Scotland, even making it his seat of government at one time, locking up prisoners in the keep and generally behaving like a proper in-your-face king. After his death, however, (I know, we haven't got there yet – be patient) and the accession of his son, things turned against the English, so much so that in 1315 Robert the Bruce actually laid siege to the castle. He was defeated not by the superiority of the English soldiers but by the weather. The Cumbrian rain did for him, clogging up his siege engines with mud and generally making life so unpleasant that after seven days he took his Jock army back home to rebuild their strength with some deep-fried Mars bars.

Not a lot happened in Carlisle Castle for the next couple of hundred years until in 1568 Mary Queen of Scots came to stay. Not of her own will, of course, for Carlisle was the site of her imprisonment. Her gaoler was one Sir Francis Knollys, who found the task of guarding her rather troublesome. Mary was a feisty lady and did not take kindly to the restrictions that her cousin Elizabeth imposed on her. Knollys decided that his best bet lay in trying to give her certain freedoms, so she was allowed to go riding, to watch her courtiers playing football on the castle green (giving rise eventually to Queens Park Rangers), and to do a spot of promenading along the outside of the castle walls. Knollys breathed a sigh of relief when Mary was taken off to more secure imprisonment in Bolton Castle.

The next Scot to darken Carlisle Castle's doors was Bonnie Prince Charlie himself, who in 1745 entered Carlisle preceded by 100 bagpipers, which was enough to make anyone surrender. Charlie only stayed for a few days then he was off down south, reaching Derby before everything went pear-shaped. After the subsequent Battle of Culloden, when the English forces defeated the Bonnie Prince, 382 Jacobite prisoners were sent for trial to

Carlisle Castle, many of them incarcerated in the keep with little food or water and with no daylight. Twenty of them were later tied on black hurdles and dragged through the streets of Carlisle to the English gate, where they were hanged on the gallows, then had their entrails burnt and their heads chopped off, in the cheery way things were done then.

One of those imprisoned and awaiting death is alleged to have said the following words to his visiting sweetheart:

> *"Ye'll tak the high road and I'll tak the low road, and I'll be in Scotland afore ye."*

The high road he meant was the main road back to Scotland; the low road was the road to the grave. What he didn't know, of course, was that he was creating the first two lines of another excuse for drunken Scotsmen the world over to bawl their lungs out late at night in order to tell anyone who was within earshot that they really, honestly, truly came from Loch Lomond.

The underpass that takes you from Carlisle Castle to Tullie House Museum under the thunderingly noisy main road south is adorned with the names of the Border Reivers, so you can walk all over those Armstrongs, Bells, Johnstones, Scotts, Elliott, Nicksons, Kerrs, Dodds, Douglases, Regans and Grahams in ways that you wouldn't have dared several centuries ago

Tullie House Museum is a relatively recent development on its present site. It really is quite sumptuous, telling the story of the Borders area from its Ice Age beginnings to the modern day in a variety of striking ways, using modern technology, imaginative reconstructions and thoughtful placing and displaying of historical finds.

At its centre, inevitably, is a display about Hadrian's Wall and the Roman conquest, introduced very powerfully by the

Conquest Stone, a carving found in the wall of Stanwix church in Carlisle in 1787 which depicts a Roman cavalryman riding over the naked body of a native Briton. This was used as Roman political propaganda to demonstrate the Roman Empire subduing the barbarian population, and it certainly does that. Imagine, if you will – and, as I write, you don't have to imagine too hard – an American soldier leading a blindfolded Iraqi prisoner on a chain and you'll have the same sense of what was going on. The description of the Wall, with its Vallum, ditch, forts, milecastles, turrets et cetera, is rather mundane after that startling introduction but hold on, there's lots more of interest in Tullie House.

Many small items give a good purchase on what life in and under the Roman army was like – the belt buckles, sword sheaths, shoes and helmet parts. In one case there's a wooden training sword, miraculously preserved, which is exactly the same dimensions as the short iron sword used in battle by the troops. This would have been like those used in the *basilica exercitatoria* (drill and exercise hall) at Birdoswald. In another case there are two wooden tent pegs, shaped exactly like those I used to hammer into the ground when I was in the Scouts. A further case has a range of tools – a pruning hook, a plumb-bob for drawing vertical lines, a stonemason's hammer, cobbler's tools, a plough share, axe hammers, knives, a wooden bung from a barrel. All of these so vividly bring back to life their possessors, our so-distant Roman conquerors.

You climb a short flight of steps and you're on a mock-up of the battlements on the Wall itself and there's a replica catapult, or *cheiroballista*, which is actually a smaller version of the most powerful arrow-firer in history, the *arcuballista*, which could fire up to 400 metres. And you can have a go on this crossbow-style catapult. Just point it at the sheep skull ahead of you (that's what the soldiers liked to do for practice), press the red button and boiiing! The imaginary arrow flies through the air and a recorded voice says *"Bernard"*. Or at least that's what I thought it said. So I fired again, and again, and again, by which time I'd realised that it was actually saying *"Bono"*, meaning "Good". There's another machine right next to it where you can actually shoot real peas at a target. Mind you, they only go a maximum of three feet and I'm not convinced that the Roman army used peas like this anyway, but it's great fun.

On the rampart itself there's a Roman soldier, in full uniform, willing to let you try his shield for size and suggesting you read some of the writings about a soldier's life that are written on the wall behind, such as:

> *"I give thanks that while the others are working hard*
> *all day cutting stones, I am now a principalis [N.C.O]*
> *and stand around doing nothing."*

(Letter from a soldier in Egypt in A.D.107)

Or this:

> *"Another son joined the army –*
> *Centurion bait, his brains*
> *Half-cudgelled out whenever he*
> *Leaned on his spade."*

(Juvenal)

And there are stone carvings from the Wall, the markings of the legions that built it – a sea-goat or capricorn which was the symbol of the II Augusta legion stationed in Caerleon, and a wild boar, symbol of the XX Valeria Victrix legion from Chester. Best of all is a stone floor tile which bears the stamp "LEG VIIIIH" from the missing Ninth Legion.

Down the steps again there's even more, such as a clever display behind glass of several layers of a Roman street with a two-handled jar, sandals, a cartwheel, pottery, an iron spearhead, and pipes to channel water. There are more bits and pieces to indicate everyday life in that Roman street, like an iron furniture leg, iron wheel tyres, a bronze pail, a bronze mirror and its case.

Some remarkable findings illustrate the minutiae of body-care – fine needles used for eye surgery, spatulas, ear-picks and hairpins. Finally, there are opportunities to practice mounting the saddle of a wooden horse, à la Roman cavalrymen (you can watch yourself do it in the handily-placed mirror) and to scratch something rude on a wax tablet.

It is altogether a superb exhibition and gives you a real feel for what the soldiers experienced, both on the Wall and off it. There's also a terrific film about the Border Reivers and stuff about Bonnie Prince Charlie. Go and see it – it's worth every penny. Then pop into the centre of town as I did and treat yourself to a cup of coffee and a muffin in the Costa coffee bar situated upstairs in Ottakars bookshop.

If you're really sharp, you can buy my other books there too!

I was sipping a welcome pint of Black Sheep bitter in the Cumberland Arms in Carlisle's notorious Botchergate. This was one of the pubs designed for the Carlisle State Management Scheme, i.e. the state control system set up in the First World War to run Carlisle's brewing and thus to control the drinking of the local munitions workers by introducing the silly licensing laws that continue to our day. While I was drinking, a couple of fellow walkers, John and Kevin, whom I'd met at the Abbey Bridge in Lanercost the previous evening, walked in.

"Couldn't you find any decent beer either?" I asked them, turning round from my position at the counter.

"No,' said Kevin. "The bars are all for youngsters here, aren't they? We can't stand that pressurized lager rubbish."

They ordered pints of Black Sheep and we sat down, away from the giant-screen TV which seems to be a prerequisite in city centre pubs these days, even when there's hardly anything actually being watched. It's all part of the ambient noise that is thought essential to attract today's yoof. It was clearly not successful in the Cumberland Arms. We were the only people present.

"You have to watch out for people like Paul Dodd around here," I said.

"Who's he?" asked John.

"He claims to be England's Number One football hooligan," I told them. "He's the main man in the Border City Firm."

"Is that Carlisle's fans?" asked an incredulous Kevin. "You can't imagine them having more than a few hundred, can you?"

"I know," I sighed. "But this guy travels away on England matches. Apparently he's always at the root of any trouble abroad. Remember that Northern Ireland match?"

"The one that was abandoned?" queried Kevin.

"The same," I nodded. "Dodd claims he was involved in the trouble there. He's even written a book about himself. Or at least it's 'told in his own words' by some tame journalist."

"I don't suppose he can write himself," quipped John.

"Too true," I said. "It makes the Reivers he's descended from seem like upholders of true morality by comparison, doesn't it?"

"What would Hadrian and his mob have done with him?" asked Kevin, reflectively supping from his pint of beer.

"Probably shipped him off to Rome in chains," said John.

"In the back of an Eddie Stobart lorry," I quipped. "The real king of Carlisle."

'Spotting' Eddie Stobart lorries has become a national pastime in Britain over recent years, ever since bandleader Jools Holland admitted in a Sunday Times interview that he and his band regularly competed with one another on long road journeys to get points for the number of Eddie Stobart lorries they spotted. Since then, the public appetite for the green, red and gold giants of the road has grown and grown. There are now 25,000 members in the fan club and you can buy T-shirts, baseball caps, ties, car stickers, model lorries et cetera, et cetera. Eddie Stobart's business is based in Carlisle and there is a shop in the town centre where you can, if you are really daft enough, buy all this kind of tat. I chose not to avail myself of this less-than-wonderful opportunity.

But the thought of Paul Dodd and his like being hauled away in chains in the back of an Eddie Stobart lorry did my heart good and I left my companions to head off for an evening meal in the Casa Romana ("Cumbria's Top Italian Restaurant") which my landlady at the East View Guest House, Julie Glease, had recommended. According to the legend outside, the Casa Romana was voted in the Top Ten PAPA (Pasta and Pizza) Restaurants in 1997 and I bet you didn't even know there was such a competition. You learn something new everyday, eh?

The menu announces that "Not all Italians know how to cook but they all know how to eat" and I have to say I was fêted well that evening. The *agnello arresto* (saddle of lamb) with Tuscan vegetables in a redcurrant and rosemary sauce was out of this world. I even treated myself to some real Italian ice cream for dessert and washed it all down with a bottle of excellent Merlot Della Venezia.

"That was a meal fit for an emperor," I told Toto, the small and perfectly-formed proprietor, who noisily and jovially was keeping an eye on proceedings from his desk in the centre of the restaurant.

"Si," he said. "You want a brandy? Liqueur?"

"No," I said. "I'm absolutely stuffed. Which part of Italy are you from?"

"Sicily," Toto said proudly.

"You the Carlisle Mafia?" I asked grinning.

"Sure thing," he said. "You know what is the Sicilian's favourite dish?"

"No."

"Broken leg of lamb," Toto chortled. "You get?"

"I get," I said.

"You sure no brandy?"

"I'm sure," I said again, shaking my head. "I have a long stretch tomorrow. I'd better go."

And so I settled my bill and walked back to my comfortable room in the East View Guest House to rest before my final day's walk and the completion of my journey on the Hadrian's Wall Path.

XII
HADRIAN THE BLOKE

We sometimes forget how much the average height of the human race has increased over the centuries, largely through better diet. Although the height qualification for the Roman army was almost six feet, most Romans were little more than five feet high, which was another reason why they preferred to let the much taller Germans and French do their fighting for them. Hadrian was taller than average and strongly built. He kept himself in good condition by regular exercise - he was a frequent visitor to his local gym at the public baths for muscle-pumping, bodybuilding and sword-training. His hair was curly, as we can see from the statues of him that have come down to us, and, as I've pointed out earlier, he sported a nifty beard to hide his spotty complexion. He had a typically Roman nose and deep-set, close-together eyes which give little away and seem deliberately to be hiding his character.

But what are Emperors really like, beneath the fancy-Dan costumes, the peacock abundances, the glittering lights of fame and fortune? How do they behave away from the toadies who fawn on them, the courtiers who protect them, the flunkies who whisper honeyed words of praise in their perfumed ears? What do they really think when they're not having to pontificate, not having to appear all-seeing and all-knowing, not having to be careful with their words?

Hadrian was born with the proverbial silver spoon in his mouth but even he could not have foreseen that he would one day end up as Numero Uno, the Boss, the Emperor of the Roman Empire. We know that he was a bit of a lad in his adolescence. We can surmise that the reason for his marriage to Sabina was largely connected to the fact that he was caught in some hanky-panky with the boys that Trajan kept for his own pleasure. Then, having corrected his waywardness in the eyes of the public, as he no doubt thought, he got mocked for his Spanish accent when he addressed the Senate. That must have rankled and given rise to thoughts of murderous revenge on those who laughed at him.

Somewhere round about this time, Hadrian seems to have knuckled down, studying hard to make sure his Latin was top-notch (he should have had the Reverend Rust) and earning Trajan's trust by accompanying the Emperor on his battle campaigns and seemingly learning to drink like a trooper as well. From then on most of what we know of him is his career path, as he climbed the greasy pole to the ultimate top job, which he held for 21 years from Trajan's death in A.D.117 to his own demise in A.D.138.

Hadrian obviously had some sort of grand policy plan when he succeeded Trajan. He promoted himself in the public eye as a new Augustus. That's why he pulled back from extending the Empire any further east or north or south and built those boundary markers – the wooden barricades in Germany and Africa, and the Wall in Britain. Half his time as Emperor was spent travelling the furthest bounds of the Empire, ensuring that the legions were up to scratch by instituting a programme of daily training, which probably consisted of drill, exercise, training with wooden swords and marching. He made sure that all those appointed to positions of rank in the army had earned that promotion and were of appropriate age and experience, and improved the weapons and equipment of the squaddies. All evidence of luxury living, such as banqueting halls and other fancy additions to army bases, he removed. He introduced new rules for army duties and expenses, and he stopped the squaddies from going AWOL without reason. He checked that the Empire's boundaries were well guarded, and, where necessary, sought peace with the rulers of neighbouring states rather than threatening them with hostile invasion. He was the most travelled of the Roman emperors, his insatiable curiosity for knowledge about the rest of the world matching well his ambitions to ensure that the Empire's boundaries were fixed and secured.

In Rome Hadrian had the political good sense to realise that killing four of his enemies in the Senate on his accession would not play well with the populace of Rome, so he gave every citizen a substantial cash gift and cancelled private debts to the state. He also gave liberally to senators who had fallen on hard times, made himself highly visible by attending loads of official functions, and gave generously of his time to visit the sick and lame. A series of legal reforms was initiated by him which sought to combine justice with human kindness and brought together many of the laws which were to form the basis of the great Roman system of law which in many ways is the greatest gift that the Romans handed on to succeeding generations. He initiated huge building progammes in the capital city, notably the rebuilt Pantheon described earlier.

But what was he really like as a bloke?

Well, he wasn't exactly a blokey sort of bloke. Sure, he could demonstrate physical courage and strength, marching ahead of his troops on 20-mile route marches with no hat and fully armed, both in the Egyptian deserts and in the winter snows of Germany. He even shared meals of cheese and bacon with the squaddies in the Roman NAAFI. Allegedly he was also skilled in gladiatorial combat, though it's hard to see how he would have practiced this, when the gladiators were of a different class to him, and usually died in combat. His prowess as a huntsman was legendary, from his teenage years in Spain to the momentous lion-hunt in Egypt with Antinous when he was 54 years old, despite suffering a broken collarbone and rib on a previous hunting expedition. And he survived two assassination attempts, even ensuring that the mad slave who attacked him in his garden was handed over to doctors for treatment. He also enjoyed mountaineering, skipping up Mount Etna in Sicily and Mount Casius in Syria in his middle years in order to witness the sunrise from the top.

I guess, such was the nature of the Roman hegemony, that you had to prove yourself a bit of a hard knock, so it's not too surprising that Hadrian should have chosen to do the things I've mentioned above. At the same time, however, he was obviously an egghead too. He was interested in geometry, arithmetic and painting; hence his predilection for architecture and for his grand designs such as the triumphal arch in Athens or his villa in Tibur or, let's face it, the Wall itself. He wrote some racy love poetry about the objects of his fancy and he even composed his autobiography, though sadly none of these writings have survived to our times. He painted, he played a mean guitar, he sculpted. He was a keen astrologer, for these were times when the ability to read your fortune in the stars was considered crucial.

Hadrian liked a good argument. Everywhere he went he sought out philosophers, professors, writers and teachers for a spot of verbal wrangling. He published pamphlets in which he attempted to ridicule the teachings of some of these scholars and he was not averse to dismissing them, even sending them to exile, if he felt like it. The trouble was he was two-faced about some of this. He was a questioning type of bloke who enjoyed debate but, although he professed himself distraught to see anyone with hurt feelings and although he frequently gave generous gifts and honours to these scholars, he also humiliated some of them by being waspish and mean-spirited. He clearly had a sharp tongue.

How are we to understand these apparently contradictory sides to Hadrian's nature - this bloke who was popular with his squaddies and enjoyed mucking out with them and this egghead who sought to humiliate his fellow eggheads? It is possible that he was much more at ease with those who were socially beneath him, with whom he could enjoy a joke, a splash in the public baths, a spot of marching, a basic meal, than with those of his own class, especially those who were highly educated. It's a bit like Prince Charles mouthing off about English grammar or modern architecture, about which he knows nothing. I guess both of them suffer from insecurity, being forced by their breeding to behave in quite unnatural ways in public yet also feeling the need to demonstrate intellectual powers that they were never trained to possess.

Hadrian spent half of his time as Emperor away from Rome, visiting the farthest points of the Roman Empire, officially to ensure the boundaries of that Empire were secure but perhaps unofficially because of his own inner sense of restlessness. Although his accompanying band of engineers, architects and builders were there to improve defences, to build roads, to create harbours, markets, aqueducts, and public baths, Hadrian himself clearly wanted to see and experience as much of the known universe as possible. Who wouldn't want to sample Liebfraumilch in Rhineland, to scrunch on pork scratchings in Britain, to get a sun tan in Spain, or to see the Olympic Games in Greece?

Here are two bits of seemingly contradictory behaviour from our Emperor – his favourite food was something called a *tetrafarmacum* (literally four-fold medicine) which was actually a meat pie comprising sow's udder, pheasant and ham encased in pastry. So now we know who ate all the pies. This is the sort of thing you might expect to be the favourite food of someone who spent most of his life at football matches, wouldn't you? Well, Hadrian did like his Games. Or at least he realised that, in order to keep the population of Rome happy, you had to organise a few opportunities for a good booze-up and the Games were the official excuse for that. Nothing like a few dead lions, a spot of dodgy chariot-racing, a chance to see Russell Crowe or Kirk Douglas taking on all-comers in the gladiatorial arena, then a stop-over on the way home at the handily-placed brothel just outside the Circus Maximus for a spot of rumpy-pumpy. Plus, of course, all-day drinking and as many meat pies as you could get down you.

You could see why that sort of thing might appeal to the cruder type of citizenry, but to Hadrian, our sensitive philosopher and poet? It seems unlikely, doesn't it?

But Hadrian also liked his mysteries, or should I say his Mysteries, for the Eleusinian Mysteries to which he was initiated in Greece in about A.D. 128 were the top tip for those seeking a profound religious experience in those days. The Emperor was initiated into the Eleusinian Mysteries on his visit to Greece in A.D. 128, almost certainly with his beloved Antinous by his side. For centuries the Eleusinian Mysteries had been one of the top attractions on any trip to Greece. Allegedly undergoing this experience brought about a change of consciousness – yes, we've heard all about this sort of thing in our own times, haven't we? Anyway those who participated were sworn to secrecy about what happened so what I'm about to reveal is based on my own initiation and I shall probably be excommunicated for telling, so please keep quiet about all this.

The Mysteries began with a procession from Athens to Eleusis, which was followed by a spot of ritual bathing, dressing up in new togs and fasting. Nothing unusual there. It's the sort of thing that most religions have adopted somewhere or other in their modus operandi. After all that preparation, the initiates dressed in dark robes and, carrying a wooden staff and myrtle branches (don't ask, I haven't got a clue), were led along the Scared Way across two bridges, at the first of which an old woman lifted up her skirt to give you a bit of a laugh and at the second of which you had to give your password. Then initiates were given a magic potion, made from something like magic mushrooms and therefore hallucinogenic, after which of course it's not long before you had the wonderful vision, your consciousness was changed forever and man, life was really groovy, yeah.

Good stuff, eh? No wonder Hadrian thought this was cool. Is this then some clue to his personality? Was he, as some experts argue, a lifelong mystic, who sought in the writings of the ancients and in the religious practices of those outward-lying regions of the Empire that he was intent on visiting some truth that he could not find in the gods and goddesses of Rome he had been brought up with? Was the alleged sacrificial death of Antinous another example of this longing of Hadrian for some eternal truth and understanding?

It's hard to know. It's even harder to square this lover of meat pies with this mystic seeker after the truth, this hard man who marched bare-headed at the head of his troops with the sensitive poet, this argumentative and querulous philosopher with the kind and wise ruler. Hadrian the bloke does indeed seem to have been a mass of contradictions.

> *He was, in the same person, austere and genial, dignified and playful, dilatory and quick to act, niggardly and generous, deceitful and straightforward, cruel and merciful, and always in all things changeable.*

So says his anonymous biographer, and who was I to argue with that judgement before I set off on the final stage of my trek along the line of his greatest enduring monument, the Roman Wall?

XIII
BACKSLAPPING IN BOWNESS

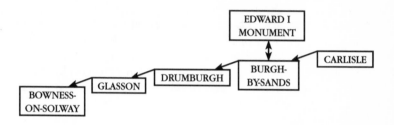

The final day of my trek began with the same warm sun that I had enjoyed for most of the week. I left Carlisle on the riverside trail that follows the River Eden past Carlisle Castle, soon passing underneath the railway bridge that carries the West Coast main line to Scotland and the trains that inspired Auden's classic hymn to the glories of steam trains, *Night Mail*. I found myself muttering those hypnotic lines:

> *This is the Night Mail crossing the border*
> *Bringing the cheque and the postal order.*

There is no sign of the Wall now but, after you leave the River Eden by the tiny village of Grinsdale, you do see the Vallum in fields to the south as you walk. After Kirkandrews the Path rejoins the riverbank to take you into the village of Beaumont, literally the 'beautiful hill'. Here St Mary's church stands on the highest point where once there was a Roman milestone. The church dates its origins to the 12th century and large parts of it were, inevitably, built with stones from Hadrian's Wall.

The Latin inscription in the Wall of nearby Hilltop Cottage has recently been identified as being the mark of a troop of North African soldiers from modern-day Morocco. There is a proposal to institute DNA testing on local people to see if there is any evidence of interbreeding between the white locals and black soldiers stationed here, probably in a working camp to build or repair the Wall. Wouldn't it be ironic if it turned out that Cumbrian BNP members were actually descended from Africans?

From the church you can see Galloway on the other side of the Solway Firth, and I was reminded that a few miles due north from Beaumont is Gretna Green, where the Old Blacksmith's Shop still conducts weddings, though they are no longer of ladder-at-the-window eloping couples. I shared William Hutton's reaction to this place:

> *"I saw Gretna Green, that source of repentance; but,*
> *being myself half a century above par, and not having*
> *with me an amorous lass of eighteen with as many*
> *thousands, I had no occasion for the blacksmith."*

Though I'm not quite the "half century above par" that he was.

Just south of Gretna stood the government munitions factory that once produced what became known as Devil's Porridge. The factory, which asserted it was the greatest munitions factory on earth, opened in 1915 and employed over 30,000 people. Amongst its claims were the following:

- Its own railway network had 125 miles of track, with 34 railway engines.
- Its own large power station provided electricity for the factory and the townships.
- It had its own water treatment plant handling 10 million gallons daily.
- Its telephone exchange handled 2.5 million calls in 1918.
- The factory bakeries produced 14,000 meals and 13,000 loaves daily.
- The laundry could clean 6,000 items daily.

Devil's Porridge was a highly explosive mixture of nitro-glycerine and nitro-cotton, which, when dried, was shaped into cordite and put into shells and bullets. The name was given by Sir Arthur Conan Doyle when he visited the factory and saw this stuff being mixed by hand.

"Good heavens, why d'you call it that?" exclaimed Watson, peering into the grey bubbling mess.

"Elementary, my dear Watson," said Holmes. "A perfect fool could tell you that, when you mix these substances together, you are playing with the devil."

"And porridge, Holmes?" pressed the good doctor, not yet convinced by the sleuth's explanation.

"Watson, do you not know that we have crossed the border and stand in the land of the thistle? And the only food the Scots eat is porridge. Hence the nomenclature the Devil's Porridge."

"I think I will stick with kippers in the morning," replied Watson.

Neither porridge nor kippers were what I hoped for when a short while later I entered Burgh-by-Sands (pronounced Bruff), where you immediately come upon 12th-century St. Michael's church, built on the site of the Roman fort of Aballava using, obviously, stones from the fort and the Roman Wall. A notice outside the church tells you that it was the last resting-place of Edward I, and a fingerpost opposite directs you to the Solway marshes where a monument to Edward is to be found. It's worth walking the extra couple of miles that this diversion entails, just to see this tall monument, surrounded by an iron fence to keep the latter-day Jocks from despoiling it, in the middle of one of the bleakest spots you could imagine.

Edward Longshanks marshalled his troops here after leaving

Lanercost, with the intention of marching at low tide across the Firth and into Scotland to take on Robert the Bruce and his kilted warriors and finish off their resistance for good. Longshanks was still not well and in July 1307 he died on this spot, struck down with dysentery. His bowels were allegedly buried in St. Michael's church in Burgh-by-Sands, presumably so the locals would be able to enjoy the smell of kingship for ever after.

Back in Bruff, I stopped for lunch in the Greyhound Arms, where I met my companions of the previous evening, John and Kevin, who had also detoured to visit Edward's monument.

"It's worth the visit," I agreed. "Remarkable really. To think old Longshanks was even contemplating taking his army across those muddy sands."

"What I want to know," said Kevin, "is why the monument says it was built in 1685 when Edward died in 1307. Where's the connection?"

"That's right," chipped in John. "It doesn't make sense."

"Maybe it was something to do with the Act of Union," I muttered and immediately knew that was a daft thing to say.

"But that was 1707, wasn't it?" said Kevin.

"I know," I wheedled. "But maybe there were some preliminary skirmishes or something."

"Just after the Civil War?" said John. "I don't remember anything about that."

They were right, of course, and I was completely mistaken. I know now, because I have it from the official archivist of the Duke of Norfolk that the monument was raised by the then Duke of Norfolk on the occasion of the sale of the Barony of Burgh to the Earl of Lonsdale in 1685. The original inscription read as follows:

> *"To the eternal memory of Edward I the most famous King of England, who died here in camp whilst preparing for war against the Scots, July 7 1307. The Most Noble Prince Henry Howard, Duke of Norfolk, Earl Marshal of England, Earl of Arundel, etc., descended from Edward I, King of England, placed this monument, 1685."*

Kevin, John and I could all have read this for ourselves, of course, except for two things. The inscription has worn badly and is not easily readable. Even worse, it was written in Latin and, despite the Reverend Rust's best efforts, I just could not remember enough to decipher it.

As I supped my pint of Marston's Pedigree bitter, my eye took in a framed poster on the wall, proclaiming Burgh Races. I stood to read the poster, which announced a Meet on April 9th 1845 and forbade any "professional Jockey, or Servant in a public training stable" from riding. There were to be several one and a quarter mile heats before the grand final and the stewards were Lieutenant Lowther, Captain Parkin and Mr Hamilton, the Clerk of the Course.

"Where did the racing take place?" I asked the barman, who had noticed my interest in the poster.

"There was a racecourse on the marshes," he told me, pulling me another pint. "They say that Red Rum trained there before his Grand National victories."

"Really?" I said. "Is the course still being used then?"

"No," he said. "Hound trailing's the thing up here these days. This is where they all meet up. We had a meet a few weeks back. We were expecting about 60 people one lunchtime and 250 turned up. It was murder. Mind you, it was good for business."

As I left the Greyhound, I glanced over towards the marshes and down towards the sea but I could see no obvious signs of the racecourse. My route was now taking me along the line of the embankment built as a sea defence to protect the ill-fated Carlisle railway line, which itself was built on top of the equally ill-fated Carlisle Canal. The latter was begun in 1819, designed to provide a better link between Carlisle and the sea at the newly-christened Port Carlisle, and for some years was very prosperous, its 18-foot wide locks enabling seagoing vessels to travel in and out of Carlisle with ease. The coming of the railways, however, did for it, and in 1854 the canal was drained and a railway line built on its bed. By 1932 that too was redundant and all that is left now is this rather fine footpath, which the Hadrian's Wall Path has now utilised.

At Drumburgh, site of another Roman fort called Concavata which, like all others on this stretch, has long since disappeared completely, the route takes you on an inland diversion to bring you through Glasson where the Highland Laddie pub stands. Allegedly Bonnie Prince Charlie stopped here for a wee dram in 1745, and since I was nearing the end of my journey, it was mid-afternoon, and it was open, I gave in to temptation and treated myself to a further pint, this time of Black Sheep Special bitter, before heading off on the last stage of my journey. Charlie wasn't there but the beer must have been having an effect because I see in my notes that I wrote the pub's name down as the Hieland Lassie. Well, he did evade capture later on in his life by dressing up as a girlie.

From Glasson a green track takes you back to the shoreline and around the edge of Port Carlisle where the canal and the railway once ran but which is now a dormitory village for Carlisle. Then it's full steam ahead for the last mile or so, with long stretches of sea and sand on your right-hand side, into Bowness-on-Solway and the end of the Hadrian's Wall Path.

Here the VI Victrix legion built the final fort on the line of the Wall, Maia, which was responsible for the northern part of the Cumbrian coastal defences that stretched from here down the western shores of Cumbria to Maryport. This was a big fort, reckoned to be the second largest on the whole Wall stretching over some seven acres. Excavations in the 1970s revealed extensive barrack blocks, inscriptions showing it housed a 1000-strong infantry garrison in the 3rd century A.D. and the fact that it was in use certainly up to the end of the 4th century, just before the Romans left England. Sadly (or gladly, if you're like Kiri and had enough of bloody Roman forts and milecastles), there's nothing of Maia visible nowadays, though a map on the outside of the King's Arms tells its story and shows how the modern village grew within the walls of the fort.

And it's with the King's Arms that the story of my journey reaches its climax, in ways that I had not anticipated.

I suppose, looking back, there was an early intimation of what was to come as soon as I entered the King's Arms and asked for my room. Dave, the landlord, took me upstairs and pointed to where I was to stay and to the bathroom opposite.

"There's no key," he explained. "People kept going away with the keys and forgetting to send them back. Anyway, walkers are honest folk. We've never had anything taken. We're all honest up here."

If only, I thought. And then had second thoughts. Dave was right. We are too obsessed with locking everything up these days. Even I, with nothing in my rucksack but dirty underpants, had been excessively careful about my possessions over the past few days, when all the evidence from the kindliness and care of the borderlands people had given me completely the opposite signals.

I washed and changed and went downstairs into the bar. I knew in advance that the pub was open all day and I had noticed a TV in the bar just inside the front door. I reasoned that there would almost certainly be a few of the locals in to watch that late afternoon's international football match in the European Championship between England and Switzerland – a match that England had to win in order to stand any chance of proceeding to the next stage of the competition. Sure enough, there were a couple of blokes in there, settling into their seats for the match, debating possibilities in the way we football-anoraks always do at such times.

"Bloody Beckham," said one lad, sipping his pint of lager. "He'd better be on form tonight. He was shite last match."

"And Owen," said his mate. "At least we've got Rooney."

Just at that moment, the front door of the pub opened and a large blond-haired Viking walked in, with a grin that split his face from ear to ear.

"Alright then, Michael?" said one of the lads.

"Has it started?" Michael asked, still grinning. "Pint please, Dave."

Honestly, all he needed was the horns. Michael was Viking Warrior incarnate. He could have stepped straight off the longboats. His ancestry was absolutely clear. And it certainly had nothing to do with the Moors of Bruff.

There was general agreement after the match was over that England had at last played up to our expectations, that the scoreline of 3-0 did not flatter them and was deserved, and that, if they continued playing like this, they were definitely going to end up as European champions. Even if we had to play the perfidious French again. This optimism may have been helped by the quantities of beer we drank. I'd intended to take it easy but, come the end of the match, I'd consumed three pints of Jennings's very wonderful Cumberland Ale. I decided I needed to soak it up, so ordered a meal of peppered steak and mushrooms, which was delicious. And another pint.

By seven thirty, I was drunk. I needed fresh air, so headed out of the King's Arms past the local primary school out of Bowness on to the seashore. It was low tide as I walked back along the strand in the direction of Carlisle. The Solway Firth is a twitcher's idea of paradise, especially in winter when huge numbers of wildfowl and waders stop off on their way to northerly feeding grounds. The sound of goose wings flapping is said to be the sound of the Solway. Further along the Firth from Bowness the Royal Society for the Protection of Birds manages Campfield Marsh to provide feeding for wintering geese, and regularly you can see thousands of such birds on the Firth or in the marsh. As I walked, I saw a long-legged heron being chased off some prime spot of beach by an angry gull, further along a gang of sandpipers was scurrying around hunting for flies and worms, and a couple of brightly-plumed oystercatchers skimmed low across the sea's edge.

The sky was huge, azure blue and stretching into infinity in the evening sun. I came up from the sand by some steps that brought me to a place known as The Banks, where there is a small shelter and the final stamping place for the Hadrian's Wall Path Passport holders. A small gathering of other walkers were already there, all of them people I had met at some point on my journey. We congratulated each other on our achievement with some traditional hand-shaking and back-slapping. When they'd all gone, I sat alone in the shelter and gazed out to sea. There are plans to create interpretive panels on The Banks, to show the history of the area, from Viking to Roman influence, through Mediaeval times to Edwardian and modern day, plus the wildlife of the area, including the bird life of the Solway Estuary and the associated inland sites of wildlife importance.

Others had been in this place before me. The soldiers of VI Victrix legion who built Maia would have no doubt stood here or hereabouts and stared out to the inhospitable lands where the woad-painted Picts lived. The Viking settlers who came in from the west would have gazed around them here and seen the fertile lands to the south and the Solway Firth to the north and felt at home. Anglo-Norman soldiers were certainly in Carlisle and may have ventured west to suss out the lie of the land and the possibility of seaborne attacks. Edward Longshanks's soldiers would have been here too, almost certainly, protecting their left flank against surprise attacks or looking for provisions for the troops. The quiet settlers of the Middle Ages would have looked anxiously to the Debateable Lands northwards of them and prayed that the Border Reivers wouldn't think to spread so far west in search of booty. And if Bonnie Prince Charlie had really stopped off in Glasson for a glass or two at the Highland Laddie, it was not beyond the bounds of belief for him to have called in at the King's Arms as well.

Although it was still early, no more than nine o'clock as I remember, I felt simultaneously euphoric and weary, so I headed back to the King's Arms to seek my bed.

"You're not allowed to sit on your own," Janice the landlady said, as I came into what was now a busy noisy bar. "It's quiz night. You've to join Pauline and Ron over there. They're one short."

"But I was just going to bed," I protested feebly and to no avail.

"No, you cannot do that," said Pauline, suddenly appearing at my side. "We're one short. You have to make up the numbers. What are you drinking?"

You see? It was no good. I had to have another pint of Cumberland Ale.

"Don't worry," she said as we sat down and I was introduced to her partner, Ron. "We usually come last. It's just a bit of fun."

Pauline is a short, middle-aged woman, with a lovely inclusive smile, who told me she had lost her husband two years previously and was glad to have Ron's company now. He was an ex-soldier who had returned to his native soil and taken up his forefathers' trade of haaf-netting. This is a peculiar form of fishing for salmon and trout using a huge, oblong-shaped net that is strung on to a wooden frame. It originates in Norway and was brought to Britain by the Viking settlers, like Michael's forefathers, some 1500 years ago. Amazingly it is still practiced on this bit of the Solway Firth exactly as those Vikings did it all that time ago. I had read about it and, although no fisherman, had been curious to see it in action.

"Will you show me if I come here again?" I asked.

"Course he will," said Pauline. "Won't you, Ron?"

Ron nodded his agreement. I bought another round of drinks. Then the quiz started. This wasn't an inter-pub quiz, this was an entertainment for the locals. The first question was who was the writer of *The African Queen*, which I knew to be C.S. Forester; the second question was who were the father and daughter that starred in *On Golden Pond*, which I knew to be Henry and Jane Fonda. But that was it. I didn't know the answers to any of the other questions. I was complete crap. I think that Pauline and Ron had been told that I was a writer and been under the impression that they could sneak me into their team as a ringer. How wrong they were! True, we didn't finish last. We finished last but one. To this day I have no memory of what time the quiz finished or of how much more beer I drank that evening. I suspect it was, respectively, very late and too much. Somehow or other I found my room and tumbled into bed.

XIV
CONCLUSION

Next morning, believe it or not, I was right as rain. No hangover. No memory. No money. Well, not strictly true, but certainly there was less in my pocket than I'd started the evening with, but what the hell! I'd had a great time, being accepted by the good folk of Bowness into their company for the evening.

"It's not just good for business, the Hadrian's Wall Path," Dave explained to me, as I was sitting in a back room after breakfast perusing Janice's book of walkers' comments. "It's good for the local folk too. It breaks up their conversation, because otherwise their talk is just circling about the same things."

There you have it. Profound philosophy. Seneca would have agreed, I'm sure, though Julius Caesar would have preferred to break up their bodies than their conversation.

My bus back to Carlisle was not due till mid-morning, so I whiled away the time reading the comments in Janice's book. Lots of stuff about blisters, cows, beer and so on, much of it predictable and not especially amusing. Several attempts at *veni, vidi, vici* jokes, again rarely very funny. I was surprised at how many different nationalities had already walked the Hadrian's Wall Path since it had opened the previous year; I noted comments by walkers from New Zealand, Spain, Australia, USA, Holland, Germany, and Canada. Clearly, there is some universal appeal to Hadrian's Wall and just as clearly some very good overseas marketing. Two days prior to my arrival, a 72-year-old had recorded his stay and his intention of turning round and walking back to Wallsend, where his bicycle and trailer awaited to take him back to Grimsby – a latter-day William Hutton, no less.

I bade my farewells to Janice and Dave. The King's Arms had certainly lived up to Dave's promise. My stay there had given me a further example of the wonderful kindness and warmth of these border folk – I could have stayed there forever, but I had a bus to catch and a home to return to.

I went for a brief exploratory tour of the village, particularly St. Michael's church which sits where it is believed the Roman fort's granary used to be and was inevitably constructed from stones from the fort and Wall. The church bells have an interesting story because they were taken from Middlebie church in Dumfries in retaliation for the Jocks nicking the bells from St. Michael's on one of their cross-border jaunts.

From the edge of the village you can see the remains of the railway viaduct that was constructed in 1869 to connect Bowness and Annan in Scotland. This was a remarkable structure for its time, being over a mile long and built on the treacherous sands of the Solway Firth and it was a build up of ice that caused its initial problems some years later, though it continued in use until 1921. Apparently, in the days when alcohol could not be purchased in Presbyterian Scotland on a Sunday, Jocks used to pile on to trains in Annan in order to get drunk in Cumberland. Legend has it that not all of them got home safely, some falling drunkenly into the waters and drowning.

I took a final walk out to The Banks and sat gazing out to sea. What had Hadrian thought when he got here after surveying the length of that Wall he had planned? Did he really think that this would mark forever the boundary between the barbarians and the mighty Roman Empire? And what caused the Romans to believe that they, and only they, should be the masters of their universe?

In recent years I have visited New York and Beijing, where I sense the same sort of thrusting arrogance that must have driven the Roman Empire project over all those centuries. There is a certainty in those who seek to be top dogs in the world that their cause, and theirs alone, is what the rest of the world needs. As I write, American forces are in Iraq, seeking to enforce something called democracy on an apparently unwilling populace, just as we British some centuries ago sought to impose our version of democracy on an unwilling America. The Americans call their enemies terrorists; the Romans called them barbarians. Their enemies, whether Iraqi or Scot, see themselves as freedom fighters.

I'm not fond of thrusting nations. I would not have been happy at the great expansion of the British Empire. I would have hated the Pax Romana. I dislike the current American hegemony. And I do not look forward to the forthcoming Chinese version that is sure to dominate the latter part of the 21st century. I like countries that have had their time in the sun and now want to sit back and wallow in the comfort that has been created. I like their quietude, their respecting of the past, their sense of composure.

What I found from my journey through time was a better understanding of Roman times than my schooling was ever able to give me, but that was largely I guess because I was too young to have had any grasp of the monumental forces that shaped the world I have inhabited these past 60 years. I have discovered that Hadrian was considered a good emperor and certainly in comparison with many of the others he was lily-white. He sought to turn the Roman army into a defensive force and thus bring peace at home. Hadrian's Wall is a permanent reminder of the boundaries of the Roman empire that its builder determined and, even though those boundaries changed over time, it serves to indicate how sometimes we need to mark out limits. The American poet Robert Frost wrote that "Good fences make good neighbours" and maybe in a curious way Hadrian's Wall had a similar effect.

The people of the Borderlands have witnessed much grief. From Hadrian's time till the end of the 18th century, this was territory that was fought over, fought in and fought about. The Romans, or rather their multi-cultural troops, fought the Scots. The Northumbrians fought the Celts. The Vikings fought the Northumbrians. The Anglo-Normans fought the Scots. The Reivers fought each other. But at the same time these borderers were building their farms, their churches, their pele towers, their sea defences, their barns, their pubs and their homes. And much of what they built with was the stones quarried by Hadrian's squaddies to build his amazing monument, Hadrian's Wall.

What I found on my journey was this wild and beautiful country peopled by hardy men and women who have made their peace with history, who are striving to bring up their children and live together in the best ways they know and to show kindness to strangers, welcoming them into their midst. If Hadrian's Wall binds them together, it does not constrict them. If Hadrian's legacy is made of stone, they have used that stone to build their houses and their places of worship. If this was once the limit of Empire, it is now the gateway that, when opened, can give us some understanding of that Empire and of one of its greatest, if most enigmatic, rulers – the Emperor Hadrian.

USEFUL READING INFORMATION

Alcock, Joan (1996), *Life in Roman Britain*, Batsford

Alcock, Joan (2001), *Food in Roman Britain*, Tempus

Allason-Jones, Lindsay (2000), *Roman Woman: Everyday Life in Hadrian's Britain*, Michael O'Mara Books

Anon (2000), *Segedunum Roman Fort, Baths & Museum*, Tyne & Wear Museums

Bagshaw, Richard W. (2000), *Roman Roads*, Shire Publications

Birley, Anthony (1997), *Hadrian the Restless Emperor*, Routledge

Birley, Anthony (2002), *Garrison Life at Vindolanda: a Band of Brothers*, Tempus

Birley, Robin (1977), *Vindolanda*, Thames & Hudson

Birley, Eric (1954), *Corbridge Roman Station*, HMSO

Birley, Eric (1959), *Chesters Roman Fort*, HMSO

Breeze, David (2003), *Hadrian's Wall*, English Heritage

Breeze, David J. & Dobson, Brian (2000), *Hadrian's Wall*, Penguin

Bruce, J. Collingwood (1978), *Handbook to the Roman Wall*, Hindson & Andrew Reid

Burton, Anthony (2003), *Hadrian's Wall Path*, Aurum Press

Campbell, Robin (trans.)(1969), *Seneca: Letters from a Stoic*, Penguin

Chaplin, Sid (1951), *The Lakes to Tyneside*, Collins

Davies, Hunter (1974), *A Walk Along the Wall*, Weidenfeld and Nicolson

Deary, Terry (1994), *The Rotten Romans*, Scholastic

Embleton, Ronald & Graham, Frank (2003), *Hadrian's Wall in the Days of the Romans*, Wrens Park Publishing

Ewin, Alison (2000), *Hadrian's Wall: A Social and Cultural History*, University of Lancaster

Fraser, George MacDonald (1995), *The Steel Bonnets*, HarperCollins

Grant, Michael (trans.)(1956), *Tacitus: On Imperial Rome*,

Penguin

Graves, Robert (trans.)(1957), *Suetonius: The Twelve Caesars*, Penguin

Handford, S.A. (trans.)(1951), *Caesar: the Conquest of Gaul*, Penguin

Hutton, William (1990), *The First Man to Walk Hadrian's Wall 1802*, Frank Graham

Keegan, John (1993), *A History of Warfare*, Hutchinson

Kiefer, Otto ((1969), *Sexual Life in Ancient Rome*, Panther Books

Kipling, Rudyard (1906), *Puck of Pook's Hill*, Macmillan

Lamb, Jim (2001), *Gilsland Spa: A Co-operative Centenary History*, Co-operative Society

Lambert, Royston (1984), *Beloved and God*, Weidenfield and Nicolson

Le Bohec, Yann (1994), *The Imperial Roman Army*, Batsford

Mattingly, H. & Handford, S.A. (trans) (1970), *Tacitus: The Agricola and The Germania*, Penguin

Mawson, David (2001), *Lanercost Landmarks, Wall Walkers and Watering Holes*, Anon

McGlade, David (2004), *The Essential Guide to Hadrian's Wall Path National Trail*, Hadrian's Wall Path trust

Michie, James (trans.) (1993), *Ovid: The Art of Love*, Folio Society

Quennell, Marjorie & C.H.B. (1924), *Everyday Life in Roman Britain*, Batsford

Renfrew, Jane (1985), *Food and Cooking in Roman Britain*, English Heritage

Richards, Mark (1993), *Hadrian's Wall: Vol 1 The Wall Walk*, Cicerone Press

Richmond, I.A. (1955), *Roman Britain*, Penguin

Salway, Peter (1965), *The Frontier People of Roman Britain*, Cambridge University Press

Salway, Peter (1993), *A History of Roman Britain*, O.U.P.

Scott, Walter (1906), *Guy Mannering*, Dent

Speller, Elizabeth (2002), *Following Hadrian*, Hodder Headline

Sutcliffe, Rosemary (1954), *Eagle of the Ninth*, O.U.P.

Vehling, Joseph Dommers (trans) (1977), *Apicius: Cookery and Dining in Imperial Rome*, Dover

Von Hagen, Victor (1967, *The Roads that Led to Rome*, Weidenfield & Nicolson

Wilkinson, Philip (2001), *What the Romans Did For Us*, Boxtree

USEFUL TRAVEL INFORMATION

The best and most up-to-date travel information is available from two internet websites www.nationaltrail.co.uk/hadrianswall and www.hadrians-wall.org or from any of the Tourist Information Centres.

TOURIST INFORMATION CENTRES

NEWCASTLE
128 Grainger Street, Newcastle-upon-Tyne, NE1 5AF
Tel: 0191-277-8000
Email: tourist.info@newcastle.gov.uk

Central Station, Main Concourse, Newcastle-upon-Tyne, NE1 5DL
Tel: 0191-277-8000
Email: tourist.info@newcastle.gov.uk

CORBRIDGE
Hill Street, Corbridge, Northumberland, NE45 5AA
Tel: 01434-632815*
Email: corbridgetic@btconnect.com

HEXHAM
Wentworth Car Park, Hexham, Northumberland, NE46 1XD
Tel: 01434-652200
Email: hexham.tic@tynedale.gov.uk

ONCE BREWED
National Park Visitor Centre, Military Road, Bardon Mill, Hexham, Northumberland, NE47 7AN
Tel: 01434-344396
Email: tic.oncebrewed@nnpa.org.uk

HALTWHISTLE
Railway Station, Station Road, Haltwhistle, Northumberland, NE49 9HN
Tel: 01434-322002
Email: haltwhistletic@btconnect.com

BRAMPTON
The Moot Hall, Market Place, Brampton, Cumbria, CA8 1RW
Tel: 01697-73433*
Email: ElisabethB@CarlisleCity.gov.uk

CARLISLE
Old Town Hall, Green Market, Carlisle, Cumbria, CA3 8JE
Tel: 01228-625600
Email: tourism@carlisle-city.gov.uk

* Open April to October only

MAPS

1:25,000 Ordnance Survey Explorer series:

316	Newcastle-upon-Tyne
OL43	Hadrian's Wall
315	Carlisle
314	Solway Firth

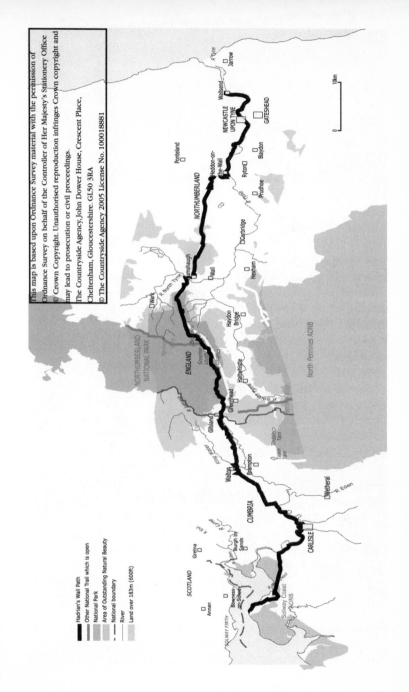

This map is based upon Ordnance Survey material with the permission of Ordnance Survey on behalf of the Controller of Her Majesty's Stationery Office © Crown Copyright. Unauthorised reproduction infringes Crown copyright and may lead to prosecution or civil proceedings.

The Countryside Agency, John Dower House, Crescent Place, Cheltenham, Gloucestershire. GL50 3RA

© The Countryside Agency 2005 License No. 100018881

Hadrian's Wall Path
Other National Trail which is open
National Park
Area of Outstanding Natural Beauty
National boundary
River
Land over 183m (600ft)

189

THE GUIDE

STARTING AT SEGEDUNUM

PLACES TO VISIT

- SEGEDUNUM ROMAN FORT, BATHHOUSE & MUSEUM
Five minutes walk from Wallsend Metro station (remember, *noli fumare*). Get your hands-on experience in the museum, see the playing-card fort outline from the Viewing Tower, clean yourself up in the bathhouse, then relax in the Flavia Café.
Open daily. Admission charge, reduced for English Heritage members.
Tel: 0191-236-9347
www.twmuseums.org.uk

□ □ □

PLACES TO EAT AND DRINK

- WALLSEND
The Anson, Station Road, Wallsend, Tyne & Wear, NE28 8QS
Tel. 0191-262-3012
Noisy town centre pub, with loads of televisions, etc, but good cheap food and decent beer. Think off-duty squaddies.

□ □ □

PLACES TO STAY

Hadrian Lodge Hotel Hotel, Wallsend, Tyne and Wear, NE28 6HH
   Tel: 0191-262-7733
   E-mail: claire.stubbs@barbox.net
   Web: www.hadrianlodgehotel.co.uk

Imperial Guest House Guest House, 194 Station Road, Wallsend, Newcastle upon Tyne, NE28 8RD
   Tel: 0191-236-9808
   E-mail: enquiries@imperialguesthouse.co.uk
   Web: www.imperialguesthouse.co.uk

HEADING FOR HEDDON

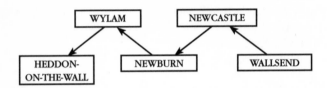

PLACES TO VISIT

- BALTIC CENTRE FOR CONTEMPORARY ART

Just across the Blinking Eye Bridge from the Quayside. Wander around and be stunned by the spectacular displays, spend money unwisely in the bookshop, have a meal (or look at the menu) and look over Newcastle from the top-floor Riverside Restaurant.

Open daily. Free admission.

Tel: 0191-478-1810

www.balticmill.com

- MUSEUM OF ANTIQUITIES

On the Newcastle University campus about two minutes walk from Haymarket Metro station. Get your introduction to the bits of the Wall our Victorian forefathers thought worth displaying, including the original Mithraeum from Brocolitia Fort.

Open daily, except Sundays. Free admission.

Tel: 0191-222-7849

www.ncl.ac.uk/antiquities

- GEORGE STEPHENSON'S BIRTHPLACE COTTAGE

About half a mile off the Path along the former Wylam Waggonway but well worth the extra bit of walking. If you've ever been fascinated by trains, this is where they were first dreamt of.

Open Thurs-Sun afternoons from Easter to late October.Small admission charge but free to National Trust members.

Tel: 01661-853457

www.nationaltrust.org.uk

- HADRIAN'S WALL, HEDDON-ON-THE-WALL

Right on the Path and not to be missed, this first big section of the Wall itself – startling to come upon.

Always there and free to see.

PLACES TO EAT AND DRINK

- BYKER

Free Trade Inn, St. Lawrence Road, Byker, Newcastle-upon-Tyne, NE6 1AP

Tel: 0191-265-5764

Small pub that looks up towards the Tyne bridges. Friendly staff and lovely atmosphere. Serves several Mordue (Co. Durham) beers and Theakstons.

- NEWCASTLE

Bridge Hotel, Castle Garth, Newcastle-upon-Tyne, NE1 1RQ

Tel: 0191-232-6400

Near to the high-level bridge, with gardens overlooking the River Tyne and the old town walls. Serves Black Sheep and Mordue Workie Ticket. Upstairs folk club.

- NEWBURN

The Keelman, Grange Road, Newburn, NE15 8ND

Tel: 0191-267-0772

Grade II listed building, formerly the water pumping station but now the home of the Big Lamp brewery. Excellent range of own beers and very tasty and filling grub. Really big garden for sitting out if the weather's fine.

- WYLAM

The Boathouse, Station Road, Wylam, NE41 8HR

Tel: 01661-853431

Friendly pub next to the railway station and one of the Tyne bridges. Offers up to eight different real ales. Food served at weekends only.

- HEDDON-ON-THE-WALL

Swan Inn, Heddon-on-the Wall, Newcastle upon Tyne, NE15 0DR

Tel: 01661-853161

Originally a manor house but converted into a pub in 1840. Winner of the Green Organisation's Civic Pride award. Serves local beers and home cooking.

Three Tuns, Military Road, Heddon-on-the-Wall, Newcastle upon Tyne, NE15 0BQ

Tel: 01661-852172

Family-run pub (and it feels just like it) that serves local beers and good grub, notably take-away Sunday lunches. Winner of Carlsberg's Best Community Pub award.

- HORSLEY

Crown and Anchor Inn, Horsley, Newcastle-upon-Tyne, NE15 0NS

Tel: 01661-853105

Nice, unfussy pub that serves terrific food and is very popular with locals for that reason. Serves a range of beers, including Bass. Very friendly landlord and landlady.

□ □ □

PLACES TO STAY

A1 Hedgefield House Hotel, Stella Road, Ryton, Tyne and Wear, NE21 4LR
Tel: 0191-413-7373
E-mail: david@hedgefieldhouse.co.uk
Web: www.hedgefieldhouse.co.uk

Belvedere, Harlow Hill, Newcastle upon Tyne, NE15 0QD
Tel: 01661-853689
E-mail: pat.carr@btinternet.com
Web: www.belvederehouse.co.uk

Clifton House Hotel, 46 Clifton Road, off Grainger Park Road, Newcastle upon Tyne, NE4 6XH
Tel: 0191-273-0407
E-mail: cliftonhousehotel@hotmail.com

Newcastle Youth Hostel, 107 Jesmond Road, Newcastle upon Tyne, NE2 1NJ
Tel: 0191-231-2570
E-mail: newcastle@yha.org.uk
Web: www.yha.org.uk

The Keelmans Lodge, Grange Road, Newburn, Newcastle upon Tyne, NE15 8ND
Tel: 0191-267-1689
E-mail: admin@biglampbrewers.co.uk
Web: http://www.biglamp.com

Wormald House, Main Street, Wylam, Northumberland, NE41 8DN
Tel: 01661-852529
E-mail: jr.craven@tiscali.co.uk

Hadrian's Rest Guest House, 7 Hexham Road, Heddon-on-the-Wall, Newcastle upon Tyne, NE15 0BG
  Tel: 0191-209-6900
  E-mail: admin@jnea.co.uk
  Web: www.hadrianswallwalk.com

Ironsign Country Restaurant, Ironsign Farm, Military Road, Heddon-on-the-Wall, Newcastle upon Tyne, NE15 0JB
  Tel: 01661-853802
  E-mail: lowen532@aol.com

Houghton North Farm, Heddon-on-the-Wall, Newcastle upon Tyne, NE15 0EZ
  Tel: 01661-854364

CHUGGING TO CHESTERS

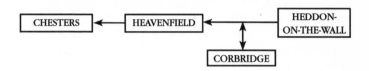

PLACES TO VISIT

- **CORBRIDGE ROMAN FORT**

A couple of miles down Dere Street off the Wall Path (check out the AD122 bus) but well worth the detour. Look out for the Corbridge Lion, marvel at the size of the granaries, walk along the Stanegate itself and dream of the arrival of the imperial postman.

Open daily April-Sept, weekends only Nov-March. Admission charge but free to English Heritage members.

Tel: 01434-632349

www.english-heritage.co.uk

- **BATTLE OF HEAVENFIELD SITE**

Learn how St. Oswald defeated the forces of darkness and brought Christianity to England (well, sort of, if you trust the Venomous Bede).

Always there and free to see.

- **HADRIAN'S WALL, BRUNTON TURRET**

A real piece of excitement for all Wall-anoraks everywhere, because here there is evidence of the ten-foot Wall and of the eight-foot Wall. Wowee!

Always there and free to see.

- CHESTERS ROMAN FORT

Right on the line of the Path, Corbridge was excavated by the father of Hadrian's Wall promoters John Clayton, one-time Newcastle Town Clerk. See the playing card shape coming to life and be amazed at the sheer size of it all. The bathhouse was the model for the Segedunum reconstruction. Museum interesting, though you need to be a bit of a boff to really appreciate it.

Open daily. Admission charge but free to English Heritage members.

Tel: 01434-681379

www.english-heritage.co.uk

□ □ □

PLACES TO EAT AND DRINK

- MILITARY ROAD

Robin Hood Inn, East Wallhouses, Stamfordham, NE18 0LL

Tel: 01434 672273

Built with stones from Hadrian's Wall this traditional pub serves a range of real ales, including Calders and Speckled Hen, and has a deserved reputation for its food, but don't expect to find any Merrie Men.

Errington Arms, Stagshaw Bank, Corbridge, Northumberland, NE45 5QB

Tel: 01434-672250

On the crossroads of Dere Street and the Military Road, with oak beams, tiled floors and open fires, this pub has a reputation for its food. Beware, though, if you want a sandwich on Sundays – full Sunday lunch only available.

- CORBRIDGE

Black Bull Inn, Middle Street, Corbridge, Nothumberland, NE45 5AT

Tel: 01434-632261

Large and comfortable mid-town pub that's always busy. Good food served all day. Beers include Castle Eden, Flowers, Boddingtons and Wadworth 6X.

- CHOLLERFORD

The George Hotel, Chollerford, Northumberland, NE46 4EW

Tel: 01434-681611

A bit posh for your average walker but of interest because of its literary associations if nothing else. Best bib and tucker if you plan to eat here, but you could try asking for Mr. Kipling's cakes!

- HUMSHAUGH

Crown Inn, Humshaugh, Hexham, NE46 4BD

Tel: 01434-681231

Recommended for its hearty, tasty, and uncomplicated food (but not on Monday or Tuesday lunchtimes). "It's the kind of place you leave with a smile on your face and a satisfied hand resting on your rounded belly. Yum!" Real ales include Theakstons.

- WALL

The Hadrian Hotel, Wall, Hexham, NE46 4EE

Tel: 01434-681232

Highly recommended, atmospheric pub with friendly staff. Good range of real ales, including Jennings, free newspapers to read, food served all day, including Sunday. Pleasant garden and lovely views.

- ACOMB

Miners Arms, Main Street, Acomb, Northumberland, NE46 4PW
Tel: 01434-603909

Open all day in summer, evenings only in winter. Amazing selection of real ales, including such wondrous-sounding beers as Durham White Velvet, Mansfield Four Seasons, and Federation Buchanan's Best. Highly-recommended home cooking, with everything fresh and reasonably priced.

The Forum, Market Place, Hexham, Northumberland, NE46 3PB
Tel: 01434-609190

Wetherspoon pub that is a converted old cinema, preserving its Art Deco style. Serves Boddingtons, Courage, Theakstons and guest beers. Non-smoking dining room where food is served all day.

Tap & Spile, Battle Hill, Hexham, Northumberland, NE46 1BA
Tel: 01434-602039

Popular pub seeking a world record for the number of different beers it has served (currently over 800). Regular live music, especially traditional Northumbrian stuff and blues.

□ □ □

PLACES TO STAY

The Barn, East Wallhouses, Military Road, Newcastle upon Tyne, NE18 0LL
Tel: 01434-672649 / 07811-060084

Wallhouses Farm, Military Road, Corbridge, Northumberland, NE45 5PU
Tel: 01434-672226

Wallhouses South Farm Cottage, Wallhouses South Farm, Corbridge, NE45 5PU
Tel: 01434-672388

Broxdale, Station Road, Corbridge, Northumberland, NE45 5AY
Tel: 01434-632492
E-mail: Broxdale@btinternet.com

Fellcroft, Station Road, Corbridge, Northumberland, NE45 5AY
Tel: 01434-632384
E-mail: tove.brown@ukonline.co.uk

Matfen High House, Nr. Corbridge, Northumberland, NE20 0RG
Tel: 01661-886592
E-mail: struan@struan.enterprise-plc.com
Web: www.smoothhound.co.uk/hotels/matfen.html

The Hayes, Newcastle Road, Corbridge, Northumberland, NE45 5LP
Tel: 01434-632010
E-mail: mjct@matthews.fsbusiness.co.uk
Web: www.hayes-corbridge.co.uk

The Riverside Guest House, Main Street, Corbridge, Northumberland, NE45 5LE
Tel: 01434-632942
E-mail: david@theriversideguesthouse.co.uk
Web: www.theriversideguesthouse.co.uk

Greencarts Farm, Humshaugh, Hexham, Northumberland, NE46 4BW
Tel: 01434-681320 / 07752-697355
E-mail: Sandra@greencarts.co.uk
Web: www.greencarts.co.uk

The Hadrian Hotel, Wall, Northumberland, NE46 4EE
Tel: 01434-681232
E-mail: david.lindsay13@btinternet.com
Web: www.hadrianhotel.com

St. Oswald's Farm, Wall, HEXHAM, Northumberland, NE46 4HB
   Tel: 01434-681307
   E-mail: ereay@fish.co.uk

Brunton Water Mill, Chollerford, Hexham, Northumberland, NE46 4EL
   Tel: 01434-681002
   E-mail: derekspqr@bruntonwatermill.freeserve.co.uk
   Web: www.bruntonwatermill.com

Alexandra, 10 Alexandra Terrace, Hexham, Northumberland, NE46 3JQ
   Tel: 01434-601954
   E-mail: sue@www.alexandrabandb.co.uk
   Web: www.alexandrabandb.co.uk

Dene House, Juniper, Hexham, Northumberland, NE46 1SJ
   Tel: 01434-673413
   E-mail: margaret@denehouse-hexham.co.uk
   Web: www.denehouse-hexham.co.uk

East Highwell House, Nr. Colwell, Hexham, Northumberland, NE46 4HX
   Tel: 01434-672235

Flothers Farm, Slaley, Hexham, Northumberland, NE47 0BJ
   Tel: 01434 673240
   E-mail: flothers@ecosse.net
   Web: www.flothers.co.uk

High Reins, Leazes Lane, Hexham, Northumberland, NE46 3AT
   Tel: 01434-603590
   E-mail: walton45@hotmail.com
   Web: www.highreins.co.uk

Laburnum House, 23 Leazes Crescent, Hexham, Northumberland, NE46 3JZ
   Tel: 01434-601828
   E-mail: Laburnum.house@virgin.net

Peth Head, Juniper, Hexham, Northumberland, NE47 0LA
   Tel: 01434-673286
   E-mail: tedliddle@compuserve.com
   Web: www.peth-head-cottage.co.uk

Rye Hill Farm, Slaley, Hexham, Northumberland, NE47 0AH
   Tel: 01434-673 259
   E-mail: info@ryehillfarm.co.uk
   Web: www.ryehillfarm.co.uk

The Queens Arms, Main Street, Acomb, Northumberland NE46 4PT
   Tel: 01434-602176

Acomb Youth Hostel, Main Street, Acomb, Hexham, Northumberland, NE46 4PL
   Tel: 0870-770-5664
   Web: http://www.yha.org.uk

Hoofing to Housesteads /
Veering to Vindolanda

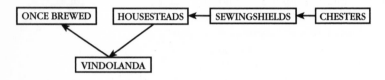

PLACES TO VISIT

- BROCOLITIA FORT & COVENTINA'S WELL

Worship at the reconstructed Mithraeum and see if you can find any of the coins that were stolen from John Clayton's original discovery of 13,487 of them. (Remember to keep your dog on a lead.)

Always there and free to see.

- HOUSESTEADS ROMAN FORT

The granddaddy of the forts on the Wall, an *"ancient splendour in bold characters"* according to William Hutton. Splendid views over the crags at the back of the fort give a sense of how the Roman army terrified the Jocks. You must, simply must, see the Roman lavatories (take your own sponge).

Open daily. Admission charge but free to English Heritage and National Trust members.

Tel: 01434-344363

www.english-heritage.co.uk

- ONCE BREWED VISITOR CENTRE

Best place for getting an overall picture of the Wall, with videos etc, and also a stopping place for the AD122 bus.

Open daily Easter – November, weekends only otherwise. Admission free.

Tel: 01434-344396 / 344777

E-mail: tic.oncebrewed@nnpa.org.uk

Web: www.nnpa.org.uk

- VINDOLANDA ROMAN FORT

A must-see experience. A mile or so south of the Path but definitely worth the detour (use the AD122 bus) because of the splendid exhibition of findings from the excavations, notably the amazing pieces of discovered written text which give a real sense of the humans who were once here.

Open daily from Easter to November. Admission charge (but get joint ticket for Roman Army Museum).

Tel: 01434-344396

www.vindolanda.com

□ □ □

PLACES TO EAT AND DRINK

- ONCE BREWED

The Twice Brewed Inn, Bardon Mill, Hexham, Northumberland, NE47 7AN

Tel: 01434-344534

Originally a coaching inn, dating back to the 17th century. Open all day with bar meals always available. Real Ales include Twice Brewed and Fortis stout.

- **MILITARY ROAD**

Milecastle Inn, Military Road, Hadrian's Wall, Northumberland, NE49 9NN

Tel: 01434 321372

Real ales include Castle Eden Banner and Northumberland Castles. Bar meals served all day, including speciality homemade pies (should keep you light on your feet for the rest of the day!).

- **HALTWHISTLE**

Black Bull, Market Square, Haltwhistle, Northumberland, NE49 0BQ

Tel: 01434-320463.

Oldest pub in town, built on site of medieval church house. Always has six regularly-changing real ales. Food served every lunchtime and evening with the exception of Monday (no food at all) and Sunday evening. Good menu, featuring many high quality game dishes alongside more traditional favourites.

□ □ □

PLACES TO STAY

Old Repeater Station, Carlisle Road, Grindon, Military Road, Northumberland NE47 6NQ

Tel: 01434-688668 / 0794-123-8641

E-mail: les.gibson@tiscali.co.uk

Simonburn Guest House, 1 The Mains, Simonburn, Northumberland, NE48 3AW

Tel: 01434-681321

E-mail: simonburn.guesthouse@btopenworld.com

Beggar Bog, Housesteads, Haydon Bridge, Hexham, NE47 6NN

Tel: 01434-344652/0783-677136

E-mail: stay@beggarbog.com

Website: http://www.beggarbog.com

Hadrian Lodge Hotel, Hindshield Moss, North Road, Haydon Bridge, Northumberland, NE47 6NF
   Tel: 01434-684867
   E-mail: hadrianlodge@hadrianswall.co.uk
   Web: www.hadrianswall.co.uk

The Anchor Hotel, John Martin Street, Haydon Bridge, Northumberland, NE47 6AB
   Tel: 01434-684227
   E-mail: anchorhotel@stay.uk.fsnet.co.uk

Twice Brewed Inn, Military Road, Bardon Mill, Northumberland, NE47 7AN
   Tel: 01434-344534
   E-mail: info@twicebrewedinn.co.uk
   Web: www.twicebrewedinn.co.uk

Vallum Lodge, Military Road, Twice Brewed, Northumberland, NE47 7AN
   Tel: 01434-344248
   E-mail: stay@vallum-lodge.co.uk
   Web: www.vallum-lodge.co.uk

Once Brewed Youth Hostel, Military Road, Bardon Mill, Northumberland, NE47 7AN
   Tel: 01434-344360
   E-mail: oncebrewed@yha.org.uk
   Web: www.yha.org.uk

Gibbs Hill Farm, Once Brewed, Bardon Mill, Northumberland, NE47 7AP
   Tel: 01434-344030
   E-mail: val@gibbshillfarm.co.uk
   Web: www.gibbshillfarm.co.uk

Saughy Rigg Farm, Twice Brewed, Haltwhistle, Northumberland, NE49 9PT
  Tel: 01434-344120
  E-mail: kathandbrad@aol.com
  Web: www.saughyrigg.co.uk

Strand Cottage, Main Road (A69), Bardon Mill, Northumberland, NE47 7BH
  Tel: 01434-344643 / 07833-968655
  E-mail: strandcottage@aol.com
  Web: www.strand-cottage.co.uk

Montcoffer, Bardon Mill, Northumberland, NE47 7HZ
  Tel: 01434-344138
  E-mail: john-dehlia@talk21.com
  Web: www.montcoffer.co.uk

□ □ □

Boogieing to Birdoswald/
Listing to Lanercost

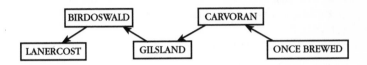

PLACES TO VISIT

- CARVORAN ROMAN ARMY MUSEUM

Three minutes from the Path off Walltown Crags. Gives a terrific idea of what it was like to be in the Roman army, stuck up there on the crags with the wind howling up your tunic. Be careful or you'll get signed up for 25 years.

Open daily from Easter to November. Admission charge (but get joint ticket for Vindolanda Fort).

Tel: 01697-747485

www.vindolanda.com

- HADRIAN'S WALL, POLTROSS BURN MILECASTLE

You go past it anyway, so you might as well have a look at the uprising steps that tell archaeologists the Wall must have been 14 feet high with a walkway on top (clever chaps, these guys).

Always there and free to see.

- HADRIAN'S WALL, HARROWS SCAR

Wonderfully-preserved long stretch of Wall approaching Birdoswald and on the line of the Path. Watch out for the Roman phallic symbols (and don't believe all the guidebooks tell you!).

Always there and free to see.

- ### BIRDOSWALD ROMAN FORT
Right on the Path itself. Interesting particularly because of the discovery of an exercise and drill hall, unique in Britain, and the remains of the East Gate are some of the best preserved on the Wall. Just as interesting as the Roman stuff, however, is the fact that the site was regularly plundered by the Border Reivers.

Open March-Nov. Admission charge.

Tel: 01697-747602

www.birdoswaldromanfort.org

- ### HADRIAN'S WALL, PIKE HILL SIGNAL TOWER
Again on the line of the Path, though not on the line of the Wall itself. Positioned to give good views over the countryside north and south and an indicator of the sort of long-distance signalling network used by the Romans.

Always there and free to see.

- ### LANERCOST PRIORY
A mile off the Path but one of the AD122 bus stops. Visible remains of the Priory a bit thin but go into the church to find out about Edward "Hammer of the Scots" Longshanks's time there and its subsequent grim history – absolutely fascinating.

Open Easter to Nov. Admission charge but free to English Heritage members.

Tel: 01697-73030

www.english-heritage.co.uk

PLACES TO EAT AND DRINK

- **GREENHEAD**

The Greenhead Hotel, Greenhead, Brampton, Cumbria, CA8 7HB

Tel: 01697-747411

Very popular with Pennine Way walkers because of being at the end of a day's walk from Alston. Open all day and serving food all day. Beers include Greene King IPA.

- **GILSLAND**

Samson Inn, Gilsland, Cumbria, CA8 7DR

Tel: 01697-747220

Small, friendly pub that serves bar meals at lunchtimes (summer only) and evenings, specialising in prize-winning Cumberland sausage and steak and kidney pies. Look out for the leek-growing championships.

Bridge Inn, Gilsland, Brampton, Cumbria, CA8 7BE

Tel: 01697-747353

Serves bar meals and snacks on summer lunchtimes and evenings only.

Station Hotel, Gilsland, Brampton, Cumbria, CA8 7DS

Tel: 01697-747338

Serves bar meals and snacks evenings only.

- **LANERCOST**

Abbey Bridge Inn, Lanercost, Brampton, Cumbria CA8 2HG

Tel: 01697-72224

Now closed – owner using inn as private residence.

□ □ □

PLACES TO STAY

Broomshaw Hill Farm, Willia Road, Haltwhistle, Northumberland, NE49 9NP
  Tel: 01434-320866
  E-mail: stay@broomshaw.co.uk
  Web: www.broomshaw.co.uk

Centre of Britain Hotel and Restaurant, Main Street, Haltwhistle, Northumberland, NE49 0BH
  Tel: 01434-322422
  E-mail: hotel@centre-of-britain.org.uk
  Web: www.centre-of-britain.org.uk

Grey Bull Hotel, Main Street, Haltwhistle, Northumberland, NE49 0DL
  Tel: 01434-321991
  E-mail: PamGreyB@aol.com
  Web: www.vizual4u.co.uk/greybull.htm

Hall Meadows, Main Street, Haltwhistle, Northumberland, NE49 0AZ
  Tel: 01434-321021

The Mount, Comb Hill, Haltwhistle, Northumberland, NE49 9NS
  Tel: 01434-321075
  E-mail: the-mount@talk21.com

Four Wynds, Longbyre, Greenhead, Cumbria, CA8 7HN
  Tel: 01697-747330
  E-mail: rozhadrianswall@aol.com
  Web: www.bed-breakfast-hadrianswall.com

Holmhead Guest House, Thirlwall Castle Farm, Hadrian's Wall, Greenhead, Northumberland CA8 7HY
  Tel: 01697-747402
  Web: www.bandbhadrianswall.com

Greenhead Youth Hostel, Greenhead, Northumberland, CA8 7HG
Tel: 0870-770-5842
E-mail: greenhead@yha.org.uk
Web: www.yha.org.uk

Braeside, Banktop, Greenhead, Northumberland, CA8 7HA
Tel: 01697-747443
E-mail: smpotts@talk21.com
Website: http://www.braeside-banktop.co.uk

Bush Nook Guest House, Upper Denton, Gilsland, Cumbria, CA8 7AF
Tel: 01697-747194
E-mail: info@bushnook.co.uk
Web: www.bushnook.co.uk

Howard House, Gilsland, Cumbria, CA8 7AJ
Tel: 01697-747285
E-mail: elizabeth@howardhousefarm.fstnet.co.uk

Slack House Organic Farm, Gilsland, Brampton, Cumbria, CA8 7DB
Tel: 01697-747351
E-mail: slackhousefarm@lineone.net
Web: www.slackhousefarm.co.uk

The Working Dales Pony Centre, Clarks Hill Farm, Gilsland, Cumbria, CA8 7DF
Tel: 01697-747208
Web: www.working-dales-ponies.com

The Hill on the Wall, Gilsland, Brampton, Cumbria, CA8 7DA
Tel: 016977 47214
E-mail: Info@hadrians-wallbedandbreakfast.com
Web: www.hadrians-wallbedandbreakfast.com

Gilsland Spa Hotel, Gilsland, Brampton, Cumbria, CA8 7AR
 Tel: 01697-747203
 E-mail: reception@gilslandspahotel.fsnet.co.uk
 Web: www.gilslandspa.co.uk

Birdoswald Youth Hostel, Birdoswald Roman Fort, Gilsland, Cumbria, CA6 7DD
 Tel: 0870-770-0124
 E-mail: greenhead@yha.org.uk
 Web: www.yha.org.uk

Quarry Side, Banks, Brampton, Cumbria, CA8 2JH
 Tel: 016977 2538
 E-mail: elizabeth.harding@btinternet.com

South View, Banks, Brampton, Carlisle, Cumbria, CA8 2JH
 Tel: 016977 2309
 E-mail: sandrahodgson@southviewbanks.f9.co.uk
 Web: www.southviewbanks.f9.co.uk

Hullerbank, Talkin, Brampton, Cumbria, CA8 1LB
 Tel: 016977 46668
 E-mail: info@hullerbank.freeserve.co.uk
 Web: www.hullerbanknb.co.uk

Kirby Moor Country House Hotel, Brampton, Cumbria, CA8 2AB
 Tel: 016977 3893
 E-mail: info@thekirbymoor-hotel.com
 Web: www.kirbymoor-hotel.com

New Mills House, Brampton, Carlisle, Cumbria, CA8 2QS
 Tel: 01697-73376
 E-mail: newmills@btinternet.com
 Web: www.newmillshouse.co.uk

□ □ □

Cross Country to Carlisle

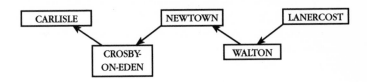

PLACES TO VISIT

- TULLIE HOUSE MUSEUM

Five minutes walk from the Path in the centre of Carlisle but a splendid experience. Climb on a reconstruction of the Wall, fire a Roman catapult, look at the tools left behind when the Legions marched off, then watch a film of the Border Reivers.

Open daily. Admission charge.

Tel: 01228-534781

www.tulliehouse.co.uk

- CARLISLE CASTLE

Also five minutes from the Path but towering over the horizon and deserving of a visit. Play football with Mary Queen of Scots, tune your bagpipes up for Bonnie Prince Charlie, or learn the origins of "Loch Lomond".

Open daily. Admission charge but free to English Heritage members.

Tel: 01228-591922

www.english-heritage.co.uk

PLACES TO EAT AND DRINK

- **WALTON**

Centurion Inn, Walton, Brampton, Cumbria, CA8 2DH

Tel: 01697-72438

The owner also runs Border County Foods, is passionate about his Cumberland sausages and his life's work is to make the best. Roaring fires, good range of real ales, including Jennings, in this "Countryside Pub of the Year".

- **LAVERSDALE**

The Sportsman Inn, Laversdale, Nr. Carlisle, Cumbria, CA6 4PJ

Tel: 01228-573255

Recently refurbished, this 18th century inn has all the traditional trappings of beams, whitewash, etc, plus its own ghost. Open all day every day except Monday. Food in the restaurant. Landlord will pick you up and drop you back on the Path.

- **IRTHINGTON**

Salutation Inn, Irthington, Carlisle, Cumbria, CA6 4NJ

Tel: 01697-72310

Has a reputation for good food served evenings only. Advisable to book. Range of real ales includes Thwaites and Hesket Newmarket.

- **CROSBY**

The Stag Inn, Crosby-on-Eden, Carlisle, Cumbria, CA6 4QN

Tel: 01228-573210

Very pleasant, comfy village pub, serving tasty lunchtime and evening food, plus Jennings beers. Deserves support because the flooding of winter 2005 devastated it.

- CARLISLE

Cumberland Arms, 32 Botchergate, Carlisle, CA1 1QS
   Tel: 01228-536900
   Conveniently placed in the centre of town, this is one of the
pubs designed for the Carlisle State Management Scheme (i.e. the
state control system set up in the First World War to run Carlisle's
brewing). It has an elegant Tudor-style exterior – just the sort of
civilised architecture intended to mirror civilised drinking which
was one of the aims of the Scheme. Good range of real ales.

PLACES TO STAY

Centurion Inn, Walton, Brampton, Cumbria, CA8 2DH
   Tel: 01697-72438 / 07976-810369
   E-mail: jackie@oldvic.force9.co.uk
   Web: www.centurion@hadrianswall.com

Townhead Farm, Walton, Brampton, Cumbria, CA8 2DJ
   Tel: 01697-72730
   E-mail: armstrong_townhead@hotmail.com
   Web: www.town-head-farm.co.uk

Walton High Rigg, Walton, Brampton, Cumbria, CA8 2AZ
   Tel: 01697-72117
   E-mail: mounsey_highrigg@hotmail.com
   Web: www.waltonhighrigg.co.uk

Vallum Barn, Irthington, Carlisle, Cumbria, CA6 4NN
   Tel: 01697-742478
   E-mail: vallumbarn@tinyworld.co.uk
   Web: www.vallumbarn.co.uk

Corbett House, Irthington, Cumbria, CA6 4NN
  Tel: 01697-741533
  E-mail: corbetthouse@tiscali.co.uk
  Web: www.corbetthouse.co.uk

The Golden Fleece Hotel, Irthington, Carlisle, Cumbria, CA6 4NF
  Tel: 01228-573686
  E-mail: edwin.fleece@fsmail.net

The Coach House, Aldingham House, Stanwix, Carlisle, Cumbria
CA3 9LZ
  Tel: 01228-522554
  E-mail: stay@aldinghamhouse.co.uk
  Web: www.aldinghamhouse.co.uk

2 Marlborough Gardens, Stanwix, Carlisle, Cumbria, CA3 9NW
  Tel: 01228-512174
  E-mail: Ian_mc_brown@hotmail.com
  Web: www.marlboroughhousebb.co.uk

Abberley House, 33 Victoria Place, Carlisle, Cumbria, CA1 1HP
  Tel: 01228-521645
  E-mail: enquiries@abberleyhouse.co.uk
  Web: www.abberleyhouse.co.uk

Aldingham House, Stanwix, Carlisle, Cumbria, CA3 9LZ
  Tel: 01228-522554
  E-mail: stay@aldinghamhouse.co.uk
  Web: www.aldinghamhouse.co.uk

Angus Hotel & Almonds Bistro Hotel, 14 Scotland Road, Carlisle,
Cumbria, CA3 9DG
  Tel: 01228-523546
  E-mail: angus@hadrians-wall.fsnet.co.uk
  Web: www.angus-hotel.co.uk

Courtfield Guesthouse, 169 Warwick Road, Carlisle, Cumbria, CA11LP
Tel: 01228-522767
E-mail: mdawes@courtfieldhouse.fsnet.co.uk

East View Guest House, 110 Warwick Road, Carlisle, CA5 1JU
Tel: 01228-522112

Langleigh House, 6 Howard Place, Carlisle, Cumbria, CA1 1HR
Tel: 01228-530440
E-mail: LangleighHouse@aol.com
Web: www.langleighhouse.co.uk

The Steadings, Townhead Farm, Houghton, Carlisle, Cumbria, CA6 4JB
Tel: 01228-523019
Web: www.thesteadings.co.uk

Carlisle Youth Hostel, Old Brewery Residences, Bridge Lane, Caldewgate, Carlisle, CA2 5SR
Tel: 0870-7705752
E-mail: dee.carruthers@unn.ac.uk
Web: www.yha.org.uk

Caldew View, Metcalfe Street, Carlisle, Cumbria, CA2 5EU
Tel: 01228-595837
E-mail: denise@caldewview.fsnet.co.uk

Backslapping in Bowness

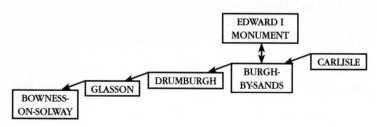

PLACES TO VISIT

- EDWARD I MONUMENT

An extra couple of miles off the Path but easy walking so go down to the marshes and see where that fearsome Hammer of the Scots, Edward I, died of dysentery. *Sic transit gloria*.

Always there and free to see.

□ □ □

PLACES TO EAT AND DRINK

- BURGH-BY-SANDS

Greyhound Inn, Burgh-by-Sands, Carlisle, CA5 6AN
Tel: 01228 576579

Conveniently situated in the heart of the village. Serves snacks all day every day but hot food only at weekends. Look out for the posters about Burgh Races.

- GLASSON

The Highland Laddie Inn, Glasson, Carlisle, Cumbria, CA7 5DT
Tel: 01697-351839

Small, friendly pub, hidden away but worth a visit. Serves food and real ales, including Jennings; closed Tuesday lunchtimes.

- PORT CARLISLE

Hope & Anchor Inn, Port Carlisle, Wigton, Cumbria, CA7 5BU
Tel: 016973-51460
Pub at the end of the canal that became a railway that became a footpath. Just off the Hadrian's Wall Path but worth a visit because it serves the exquisite Hesket Newmarket beers.

- BOWNESS-ON-SOLWAY

Kings Arms Inn, Bowness-on-Solway, Carlisle, Cumbria, CA7 5AF
Tel: 01697-351426
Absolutely the best! Most welcoming and friendly pub, open all day, serving good grub and good range of real ales, including Jennings. Stamping post for Hadrian's Wall Path Passport and keeper of walkers' legends in Janice's book. Beware of getting caught up in Quiz Night!

□ □ □

PLACES TO STAY

Vallum House Hotel, 73-75 Burgh Road, Carlisle, Cumbria, CA2 7NB
Tel: 01228-521860

Wallsend House, The Old Rectory, Bowness-on-Solway, Cumbria CA7 5AF
Tel: 016973-51055
E-mail: Patsy@wallsend.net
Web: www.wallsend.net

Kings Arms Inn, Bowness-on-Solway, Carlisle, Cumbria, CA7 5AF
Tel: 01697-351426

About Eye Books

Eye Books is a dynamic, young publishing company that likes to break the rules. Our independence allows us to publish books which challenge the way people see things. It also means that we can offer new authors a platform from which they can shine their light and encourage others to do the same.

To date we have published 60 books that cover a number of genres including Travel, Biography, Adventure, Reference and History. Many of our books are experience driven. All of them are inspirational and life affirming.

Frigid Women, for example, tells the story of the world-record-creating first all-female expedition to the North Pole. Sue Riches, a fifty-year-old mother of three who had recently recovered from a mastectomy, and her daughter Victoria are the authors – neither had ever written a book before. Sue Riches is now a writer and highly-sought-after motivational speaker.

We also publish thematic anthologies, such as The Tales from Heaven and Hell series, for those who prefer the short story format. Here everyone has the chance to get their stories published and win prizes such as flights to any destination in the world.

And here's what makes us really different: As well as publishing books, Eye Books has set up a club for like-minded people and is in the process of developing a number of initiatives and services for its community of members. After all, the more you put into life, the more you get out of it.

Please visit www.eye-books.com for further information.

Eye Club Membership

Each month, we receive hundreds of enquiries from people who have read our books, discovered our website or entered our competitions. All these people have certain things in common: a desire to achieve, to extend the boundaries of everyday life and to learn from others' experiences.

Eye Books has, therefore, set up a club to unite these like-minded people. It is a community where members can exchange ideas, contact authors, discuss travel, both future and past, as well as receive information and offers from Eye Books.

Membership is free.

Benefits of the Eye Club

As a member of the Eye Club:

• You are offered the invaluable opportunity to contact our authors directly.
• You will receive a regular newsletter, information on new book releases and company developments as well as discounts on new and past titles.
• You can attend special member events such as book launches, author talks and signings.
• Receive discounts on a variety of travel-related products and services from Eye Books' partners.
• You can enjoy entry into Eye Books competitions including the ever popular Heaven and Hell series and our monthly book competition.

To register your membership, simply visit our website and register on our club pages: www.eye-books.com.

2006 Titles

Fateful Beauty - the story of Francis Coke 1602-1642 – Natalie Hodgson
Fateful Beauty is the true story of a young woman who, at the age of 15, was forced to marry a mentally unstable man in order to fulfil the wishes of her ambitious father. It is well researched and gives a vivid picture of life at this time - political intrigue, life at court, civil war, and family and personal trauma.
ISBN 1 903070 406. £12.99.

Siberian Dreams – Andy Home
Journalist, Andy Home realises that without Norislk and its inhabitants, much of our lives in the West would need to change. So, he visits this former Prison Camp/secret city turned mining town above the Artic Circle to find out what life was really like for the 200,000 people living in sub-zero temperatures in Russia's most polluted city.
ISBN 9781903070512. £9.99.

The Good Life Gets Better– Dorian Amos
The sequel to the bestselling book about leaving the UK for a new life in the Yukon, Dorian and his growing family get gold fever, start to stake land and prospect for gold. Follow them along the learning curve about where to look for gold and how to live in this harsh climate. It shows that with good humour and resilience life can only get better.
ISBN 9781903070482. £9.99.

Desert Governess – Phyllis Ellis
A former Benny Hill Show actress becomes a governess to
the Saudi Arabian Royal Family.
ISBN: 1 903070 015. Price £9.99.

Last of the Nomads – W. J. Peasley
The story of the last of the desert nomads to live permanently
in the traditional way in Western Australia.
ISBN: 1 903070 325. Price £9.99.

All Will Be Well – Michael Meegan
A book about how love and compassion when given out to
others can lead to contentment.
ISBN: 1 903070 279. Price £9.99.

First Contact – Mark Anstice
A 21st-century discovery of cannibals.
Comes with (free) DVD which won the Banff Film Festival.
ISBN: 1 903070 260. Price £9.99.

Further Travellers' Tales From Heaven and Hell – Various
This is the third book in the series of real travellers tales.
ISBN: 1 903070 112. Price £9.99.

Special Offa – Bob Bibby
A walk along Offa's Dyke.
ISBN: 1 903070 287. Price £9.99.

The Good Life – Dorian Amos
A move from the UK to start a new life in the wilderness of
The Yukon.
ISBN: 1 903070 309. Price £9.99.

Baghdad Business School – Heyrick Bond Gunning
The realities of a business start-up in a war zone.
ISBN: 1 903070 333. Price £9.99.

The Accidental Optimist's Guide to Life – Emily Joy
Having just returned from Sierra Leone, a busy GP with a
growing family ponders the meaning of life.
ISBN: 1 903070 430. Price £9.99.

The Con Artist Handbook – Joel Levy
Get wise as this blows the lid on the secrets of the successful
con artist and his con games.
ISBN: 1 903070 341. Price £9.99.

The Forensics Handbook – Pete Moore
The most up-to-date log of forensic techniques available.
ISBN: 1 903070 35X. Price £9.99.

My Journey With A Remarkable Tree – Ken Finn
A journey following an illegally logged tree from a spirit
forest to the furniture corner of a garden centre.
ISBN: 1 903070 384. Price £9.99.

Seeking Sanctuary – Hilda Reilly
Western Muslim converts living in Sudan.
ISBN: 1 903070 392. Price £9.99.

Lost Lands Forgotten Stories – Alexandra Pratt
The retracing of an astonishing 600 mile river journey in 1905
in 2005.
ISBN: 1 903070 368. Price £9.99.

Jasmine and Arnica – Nicola Naylor
A blind woman's journey around India.
ISBN: 1 903070 171. Price £9.99.

Touching Tibet – Niema Ash
A journey into the heart of this intriguing forbidden land.
ISBN: 1 903070 18X. Price £9.99.

Behind the Veil – Lydia Laube
A shocking account of a nurse's Arabian nightmare.
ISBN: 1 903070 198. Price £9.99.

Walking Away – Charlotte Metcalf
A well-known film maker's African journal.
ISBN: 1 903070 201. Price £9.99.

Travels in Outback Australia – Andrew Stevenson
In search of the original Australians – the Aboriginal People.
ISBN: 1 903070 147. Price £9.99.

The European Job – Jonathan Booth
10,000 miles around Europe in a 25-year-old classic car.
ISBN: 1 903070 252. Price £9.99.

Around the World with 1000 Birds – Russell Boyman
An extraordinary answer to a mid-life crisis.
ISBN: 1 903070 163. Price £9.99.

Cry from the Highest Mountain – Tess Burrows
A climb to the point furthest from the centre of the earth.
ISBN: 1 903070 120. Price £9.99.

Dancing with Sabrina – Bob Bibby
A journey along the River Severn from source to sea.
ISBN: 1 903070 244. Price £9.99.

Grey Paes and Bacon – Bob Bibby
A journey around the canals of the Black Country.
ISBN: 1 903070 066. Price £7.99.

Jungle Janes – Peter Burden
Twelve middle-aged women take on the Jungle. As seen on
Channel 4.
ISBN: 1 903070 05 8. Price £7.99.

Travels with my Daughter – Niema Ash
Forget convention, follow your instincts.
ISBN: 1 903070 04 X. Price £7.99.

Riding with Ghosts – Gwen Maka
One woman's solo cycle ride from Seattle to Mexico.
ISBN: 1 903070 00 7. Price £7.99.

Riding with Ghosts: South of the Border – Gwen Maka
The second part of Gwen's epic cycle trip through the
Americas.
ISBN: 1 903070 09 0. Price £7.99.

Triumph Round the World – Robbie Marshall
He gave up his world for the freedom of the road.
ISBN: 1 903070 08 2. Price £7.99.

Fever Trees of Borneo – Mark Eveleigh
A daring expedition through uncharted jungle.
ISBN: 0 953057 56 9. Price £7.99.

Discovery Road – Tim Garrett and Andy Brown
Their mission was to mountain bike around the world.
ISBN: 0 953057 53 4. Price £7.99.

Frigid Women – Sue and Victoria Riches
The first all-female expedition to the North Pole.
ISBN: 0 953057 52 6. Price £7.99.

Jungle Beat – Roy Follows
Fighting terrorists in Malaya.
ISBN: 0 953057 57 7. Price £7.99.

Slow Winter – Alex Hickman
A personal quest against the backdrop of the war-torn
Balkans.
ISBN: 0 953057 58 5. Price £7.99.

Tea for Two – Polly Benge
She cycled around India to test her love.
ISBN: 0 953057 59 3. Price £7.99.

Traveller's Tales from Heaven and Hell – Various
A collection of short stories drawn from a nationwide
competition.
ISBN: 0 953057 51 8. Price £6.99.

More Traveller's Tales from Heaven and Hell – Various
A second collection of short stories.
ISBN: 1 903070 02 3. Price £6.99.

A Trail of Visions: Route 1 – Vicki Couchman
A stunning photographic essay.
ISBN: 1 871349 338. Price £14.99.

A Trail of Visions: Route 2 – Vicki Couchman
A second stunning photographic essay.
ISBN: 0 953057 50 X. Price £16.99.